Grade 2

2nd Grade MATH WORKBOOK
ADDITION and
SUBTRACTION

Master 1000+ Tasks and Word Problems
with Mazes, CogAT® Test Prep, and More!

Want Free Extra Goodies for Your Student?

Email us at: info@homerunpress.com

Title the email

"2nd Grade Math Workbook Addition & Subtraction"

and we'll send some extra worksheets your way!

We create our workbooks with love and great care.
For any issues with your workbook, such as printing errors, typos, faulty binding, or something else,
please do not hesitate to contact us at: info@homerunpress.com
We will make sure you get a replacement copy immediately.

THANK YOU!

First published in the USA 2020.   ISBN 9781952368059

Table of Contents

Table of Contents

Table of Contents

Table of Contents

Kids learn and stay engaged, thanks to puzzles, mazes, word problems, along with challenging math problems, and gain the confidence to improve their math comprehension and testing.

These activities are perfect for daily practice, morning work, homework, math centers, early finishers, test preparation, assessment, or for struggling students.

They will work great in 1st Grade to challenge students. They are perfect in 2nd Grade to understand and master addition and subtraction, but they also might work in 3rd-4th Grades as a review or for those who are struggling with math.

Hi. I'm Sunny. For me, everything is an adventure. I am ready to try anything, take chances, see what happens - and help you try, too! I like to think I'm confident, caring and have an open mind. I will cheer for your success and encourage everyone! I'm ready to be a really good

I've got a problem. Well, I've always got a problem. And I don't like it. It makes me cranky, and grumpy, impatient and the truth is, I got a bad attitude. There. I said it. I admit it. And the reason I feel this way? Math! I don't get it and it bums me out. Grrrr!

Not trying to brag, but I am the smartest Brainer that ever lived - and I'm a brilliant shade of blue. That's why they call me Smarty. I love to solve problems and I'm always happy to explain how things work - to help any Brainer out there! To me, work is fun, and math is a blast!

I scare easily. Like, even just a little ...Boo! Oh wow, I've scared myself! Anyway, they call me Pickles because I turn a little green when I get panicky. Especially with new stuff. Eek! And big complicated problems. Really any problem. Eek! There, I did it again.

Hi! Name's Pepper. I have what you call a positive outlook. I just think being alive is exciting! And you know something? By being friendly, kind and maybe even wise, you can have a pretty awesome day every day on this amazing planet.

A famous movie star once said, "I want to be alone." Well, I do too! I'm best when I'm dreaming, thinking, and in my own world. And so, I resist! Yes, I resist anything new, and only do things my way or quit. The rest of the Brainers have math, but I'd rather have a headache and complain. Or pout.

1. <u>Circle</u> the correct answer.

I have a series of numbers: 6, 7, 9, 12, __. <u>What</u> is the next number?

   a) 16   b) 17   c) 14

2. My brother and I played ⬚30⬚ games. If my brother played ⬚10⬚ games, <u>how many games</u> did I play?

<u>Circle</u> your answer.   a) 21   b) 40   c) 20

3. <u>Write</u> the missing numbers.

___ + ___ + ___ + ___ = 6245   ___ + ___ + ___ = 824

___ + ___ + ___ + ___ = 9531   ___ + ___ + ___ = 736

___ + ___ + ___ + ___ = 1025   ___ + ___ + ___ = 125

___ + ___ + ___ + ___ = 5378   ___ + ___ + ___ = 691

___ + ___ + ___ + ___ = 4204   ___ + ___ + ___ = 598

___ + ___ + ___ + ___ = 4137   ___ + ___ + ___ = 920

___ + ___ + ___ + ___ = 5557   ___ + ___ + ___ = 269

___ + ___ + ___ + ___ = 8734   ___ + ___ + ___ = 926

Hint:
Write the smaller number under the larger number;
Ones under ones, tens under tens;
Subtract ones, then tens.

20 - 9

10   10

Decompose 20.
20 is 10+10.

Wait...
10 + 10 – 9 =
10 + 1 = 11.

tens ones

```
   2    0
-       9
   ‾    ‾
```

In columns we subtract 9 ones out of 0 ones.

Step 1: If I subtract in columns, I need one more row above 20.

tens ones

```
   ‾    ‾
   2    0
-       9
   ‾    ‾
```

Step 2: I borrow 1 ten out of the 2 tens since 20=10+10.

tens ones
```
   1    10
   2    0
-       9
   ‾    ‾
```

Write 10 above 0 in one's place leaving 1 above 2 in ten's place.

Step 3: Cross out 2 and 0 to avoid mistakes.

Step 4: Subtract 9 ones from 10 ones: 10-9=1.

Step 5: Subtract tens, but since you have no tens to subtract, rewrite 1 ten in your answer.

tens ones
```
   1    10
   2̶    0̶
-       9
   ‾    ‾
   1    1
```

1. <u>Subtract.</u>

$$\begin{array}{r} \bar{2}\,\bar{0} \\ -\quad 9 \\ \hline \end{array} \qquad \begin{array}{r} \bar{5}\,\bar{0} \\ -\quad 9 \\ \hline \end{array} \qquad \begin{array}{r} \bar{9}\,\bar{0} \\ -\quad 7 \\ \hline \end{array} \qquad \begin{array}{r} \bar{6}\,\bar{0} \\ -\quad 8 \\ \hline \end{array} \qquad \begin{array}{r} \bar{2}\,\bar{0} \\ -\quad 4 \\ \hline \end{array}$$

$$\begin{array}{r} \bar{4}\,\bar{0} \\ -\quad 6 \\ \hline \end{array} \qquad \begin{array}{r} \bar{3}\,\bar{0} \\ -\quad 7 \\ \hline \end{array} \qquad \begin{array}{r} \bar{6}\,\bar{0} \\ -\quad 5 \\ \hline \end{array} \qquad \begin{array}{r} \bar{8}\,\bar{0} \\ -\quad 9 \\ \hline \end{array} \qquad \begin{array}{r} \bar{5}\,\bar{0} \\ -\quad 6 \\ \hline \end{array}$$

$$\begin{array}{r} \bar{3}\,\bar{0} \\ -\quad 9 \\ \hline \end{array} \qquad \begin{array}{r} \bar{6}\,\bar{0} \\ -\quad 8 \\ \hline \end{array} \qquad \begin{array}{r} \bar{4}\,\bar{0} \\ -\quad 5 \\ \hline \end{array} \qquad \begin{array}{r} \bar{7}\,\bar{0} \\ -\quad 6 \\ \hline \end{array} \qquad \begin{array}{r} \bar{9}\,\bar{0} \\ -\quad 8 \\ \hline \end{array}$$

20 - 9 = 10   + 10 - 9 = __
| 10 + 10 |

50 - 8 = __   + __ - __ = __
| 40 + 10 |

70 - 6 = __   + __ - __ = __
| 60 + 10 |

1. <u>Subtract.</u>

$$
\begin{array}{r}
^3\!\!\not4\ ^{10}\!\!\not0 \\
-\ 1\ 9 \\
\hline
2\ 1
\end{array}
$$

$$
\begin{array}{r}
\overline{7}\ \overline{0} \\
-\ 1\ 9 \\
\hline
\end{array}
$$

$$
\begin{array}{r}
\overline{3}\ \overline{0} \\
-\ 1\ 7 \\
\hline
\end{array}
$$

$$
\begin{array}{r}
\overline{8}\ \overline{0} \\
-\ 1\ 8 \\
\hline
\end{array}
$$

$$
\begin{array}{r}
\overline{5}\ \overline{0} \\
-\ 1\ 4 \\
\hline
\end{array}
$$

$$
\begin{array}{r}
\overline{4}\ \overline{0} \\
-\ 2\ 6 \\
\hline
\end{array}
$$

$$
\begin{array}{r}
\overline{5}\ \overline{0} \\
-\ 2\ 7 \\
\hline
\end{array}
$$

$$
\begin{array}{r}
\overline{6}\ \overline{0} \\
-\ 2\ 5 \\
\hline
\end{array}
$$

$$
\begin{array}{r}
\overline{9}\ \overline{0} \\
-\ 2\ 9 \\
\hline
\end{array}
$$

$$
\begin{array}{r}
\overline{7}\ \overline{0} \\
-\ 2\ 6 \\
\hline
\end{array}
$$

$$
\begin{array}{r}
\overline{7}\ \overline{0} \\
-\ 3\ 9 \\
\hline
\end{array}
$$

$$
\begin{array}{r}
\overline{9}\ \overline{0} \\
-\ 3\ 8 \\
\hline
\end{array}
$$

$$
\begin{array}{r}
\overline{7}\ \overline{0} \\
-\ 3\ 5 \\
\hline
\end{array}
$$

$$
\begin{array}{r}
\overline{4}\ \overline{0} \\
-\ 3\ 6 \\
\hline
\end{array}
$$

$$
\begin{array}{r}
\overline{6}\ \overline{0} \\
-\ 3\ 8 \\
\hline
\end{array}
$$

70 - 19 =   70 - 10 - 9 = __
> 10 + 9

60 - 25 = __ - __ - __ = __
> 20 + 5

90 - 38 = __ - __ - __ = __
> 30 + 8

1. Circle the correct answer.

I have a series of numbers: 5, 13, 21, 29, __. What is the next number?

a)   35   b)   37   c)   33

2. My brother and I ate 20 cupcakes. If I ate 13 cupcakes, how many cupcakes did my brother eat?

Circle your answer.   a)   33   b)   17   c)   7

3. Write the missing number.

___ + 600 + 10 + 8 = 5618   2000 + 200 + ___ + 5 = 2275

1000 + ___ + 20 + 3 = 1723   8000 + 100 + 30 + ___ = 8132

___ + 900 + 60 + 1 = 9961   5000 + 700 + ___ + 1 = 5741

5000 + ___ + 30 + 9 = 5039   1000 + 200 + 80 + ___ = 1280

___ + 200 + 80 + 9 = 4289   7000 + 100 + ___ + 3 = 7193

5000 + ___ + 50 + 0 = 5050   6000 + 100 + 40 + ___ = 6148

___ + 700 + 0 + 1 = 2701   4000 + 700 + ___ + 5 = 4795

9000 + ___ + 0 + 9 = 9009   1000 + 400 + 70 + ___ = 1479

Hint: Borrow from the next figure to the left;
When borrowing 1 ten, change it to 10 ones;
When borrowing 1 hundred, change it to 10 tens.

32 - 18

12   6

Decompose 18.

18 is 12+6.

Wait…

32 - 12 – 6 =

20 - 6 = 14.

In columns we subtract 8 ones from 2 ones.

tens ones

```
   3   2
-  1   8
   _   _
```

Step 1: If I subtract in columns, I need one row above 32.

tens ones

```
   ‾   ‾
   3   2
-  1   8
   _   _
```

Step 2: I borrow 1 ten from 3 tens since 30=10+20.

10 borrowed ones + 2 ones are 12 ones, write 12 above 2 in one's place. Write the leftover 2 tens above 3 in ten's place.

tens ones

```
   2   12
   3   2
-  1   8
   _   _
```

tens ones

```
   2   12
   3̶   2̶
-  1   8
   1   4
```

Step 3: Cross out 3 and 2 to avoid mistakes.

Step 4: Subtract 8 ones from 12 ones: 12-8=4.

Step 5: Subtract 1 ten from 2 tens: 2 – 1 = 1.

1. Subtract.

$$
\begin{array}{r} \bar{4}\,\bar{3} \\ -\ 1\ 6 \\ \hline \end{array}
\qquad
\begin{array}{r} \bar{7}\,\bar{1} \\ -\ 1\ 5 \\ \hline \end{array}
\qquad
\begin{array}{r} \bar{3}\,\bar{3} \\ -\ 1\ 8 \\ \hline \end{array}
\qquad
\begin{array}{r} \bar{8}\,\bar{2} \\ -\ 1\ 7 \\ \hline \end{array}
\qquad
\begin{array}{r} \bar{5}\,\bar{1} \\ -\ 1\ 5 \\ \hline \end{array}
$$

$$
\begin{array}{r} \bar{4}\,\bar{2} \\ -\ 2\ 8 \\ \hline \end{array}
\qquad
\begin{array}{r} \bar{5}\,\bar{3} \\ -\ 2\ 9 \\ \hline \end{array}
\qquad
\begin{array}{r} \bar{6}\,\bar{1} \\ -\ 2\ 7 \\ \hline \end{array}
\qquad
\begin{array}{r} \bar{9}\,\bar{4} \\ -\ 2\ 8 \\ \hline \end{array}
\qquad
\begin{array}{r} \bar{7}\,\bar{5} \\ -\ 2\ 7 \\ \hline \end{array}
$$

$$
\begin{array}{r} \bar{7}\,\bar{1} \\ -\ 3\ 5 \\ \hline \end{array}
\qquad
\begin{array}{r} \bar{9}\,\bar{3} \\ -\ 3\ 7 \\ \hline \end{array}
\qquad
\begin{array}{r} \bar{7}\,\bar{2} \\ -\ 3\ 8 \\ \hline \end{array}
\qquad
\begin{array}{r} \bar{6}\,\bar{4} \\ -\ 3\ 9 \\ \hline \end{array}
\qquad
\begin{array}{r} \bar{6}\,\bar{2} \\ -\ 3\ 6 \\ \hline \end{array}
$$

43   -   16   =   43   -   20   +   4   =   __

$\boxed{20 - 4}$

61   -   27   =   __   -   __   +   __   =   __

$\boxed{30 - 3}$

72   -   38   =   __   -   __   +   __   =   __

$\boxed{40 - 2}$

1. <u>Solve</u> the problems:

My sister has ⬚13⬚ pink ribbons, ⬚8⬚ blue ribbons, and ⬚5⬚ green ribbons. <u>How many ribbons</u> are there in all?

_____

In my class there are ⬚26⬚ kids. ⬚9⬚ kids like to read "Diary of a Wimpy Kid", and there ⬚7 fewer⬚ kids who like to read "500 Awesome Facts" than who like to read "What Should Darla Do". <u>How many kids</u> like to read "500 Awesome Facts"?

_____

<u>How many kids</u> like to read "What Should Darla Do"?

_____

Using all digits ⬚2, 5, 7⬚ write all the six different numbers possible. <u>Arrange</u> the numbers up to the greatest number.

_____

_____

1. <u>Write</u> the missing numbers $\boxed{8, 8, 9, 11, \text{ and } 14}$ to make the equation true.

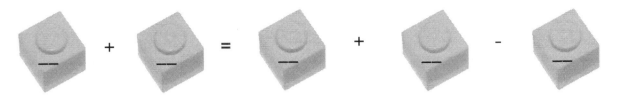

2. <u>Write</u> the missing numbers $\boxed{5, 7, 7, 8, \text{ and } 17}$ to make the equation true.

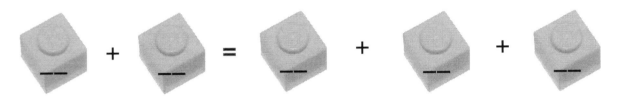

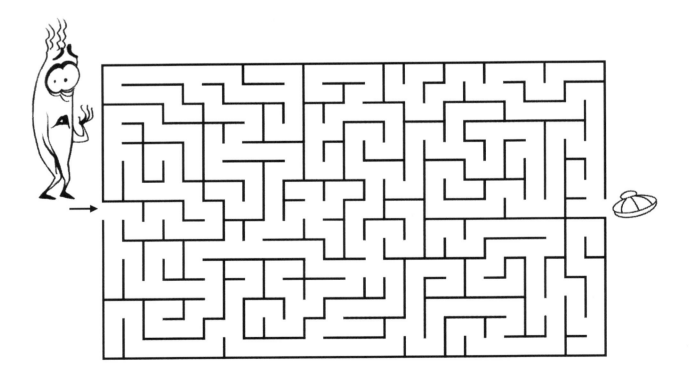

Hint: Write ones under ones, tens under tens, and so on;
Add ones first, then tens, then hundreds;
Carry when the sum in any column is 10 or more.

$$34 + 19$$

6   13

Decompose 19.

19 is 6+13. Yeah, 34 + 19 =

34 + 6 + 13 =

40 + 13 = 53.

```
tens  ones

  3    4
+ 1    9
-----------
  –    –
```

Step 1: If I add in columns, I need one more row above 34.

```
tens  ones
  ‾    ‾
  3    4
+ 1    9
-----------
  –    –
```

Step 2: First, I add ones: 4+9=13.

Write the 3 in one's place.

Carry 1 ten with the other tens.

Write the 1 above 3.

```
tens  ones
  1    ‾
  3    4
+ 1    9
-----------
  –    3
```

Step 3: Add tens: 1+3+1=5 Write the 5 in ten's place.

```
tens  ones
  1
  3    4
+ 1    9
-----------
  5    3
```

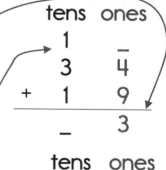

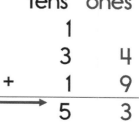

1. Add.

```
  ‾2 6        ‾6 7        ‾3 9        ‾2 4        ‾2 9
+    5      +    5      +    8      +    7      +    5
───────    ───────    ───────    ───────    ───────
```

```
  ‾3 7        ‾3 9        ‾3 4        ‾3 6        ‾3 5
+    8      +    9      +    7      +    8      +    7
───────    ───────    ───────    ───────    ───────
```

```
  ‾4 5        ‾4 4        ‾4 7        ‾4 9        ‾4 6
+    6      +    9      +    4      +    7      +    8
───────    ───────    ───────    ───────    ───────
```

29 + 6 =   29 + 1 + 5 = __
         ┌───────┐
         │ 1 + 5 │
         └───────┘

38 + 9 = __ + __ + __ = __
         ┌───────┐
         │ 2 + 7 │
         └───────┘

49 + 7 = __ + __ + __ = __
         ┌───────┐
         │ 1 + 6 │
         └───────┘

1. <u>Add.</u>

$$\overline{5}\,6 \atop +\quad 7$$ $$\overline{5}\,7 \atop +\quad 9$$ $$\overline{5}\,8 \atop +\quad 6$$ $$\overline{5}\,4 \atop +\quad 6$$ $$\overline{5}\,9 \atop +\quad 8$$

$$\overline{6}\,7 \atop +\quad 5$$ $$\overline{6}\,9 \atop +\quad 7$$ $$\overline{6}\,4 \atop +\quad 9$$ $$\overline{6}\,6 \atop +\quad 6$$ $$\overline{6}\,5 \atop +\quad 8$$

$$\overline{7}\,5 \atop +\quad 8$$ $$\overline{7}\,4 \atop +\quad 6$$ $$\overline{7}\,7 \atop +\quad 7$$ $$\overline{7}\,9 \atop +\quad 9$$ $$\overline{7}\,6 \atop +\quad 4$$

67 + 4 = 67 + 10 - 6 = __
   $\boxed{10 - 6}$

78 + 9 = __ + __ - __ = __
   $\boxed{10 - 1}$

89 + 7 = __ + __ - __ = __
   $\boxed{10 - 3}$

1. Add.

Let me help you! We have a party. You have 4 dollars (1+1+1+1). I need to give you 8 dollars back. I have only 10 dollars.

Hm... So, I have 4 dollars, you give me 10 more dollars, but I must give 2 dollars back to you, right? 28 + 10 − 2 = 38 − 2 = 36. No regrouping!

$$38 + 7 = 38 + 10 - 3 = \underline{}$$
$$\boxed{10 - 3}$$

$$54 + 8 = \underline{} + \underline{} - \underline{} = \underline{}$$
$$\boxed{10 - 2}$$

$$75 + 9 = \underline{} + \underline{} - \underline{} = \underline{}$$
$$\boxed{10 - 1}$$

2. Make and write the smallest and the biggest three-digit numbers you can with any three of these digits: 1, 4, 7, 5.

_____

1. <u>Find</u> the missing odd consecutive numbers. Consecutive numbers are numbers that follow each other in order. <u>Circle</u> the correct answer.

__, 45   a) 44   b) 42   c) 43

13, __, __   a) 12, 14   b) 14, 15   c) 15, 17

__, __, 21, __   a) 16, 17, 19   b) 19, 21, 23   c) 17, 19, 23

__, __, 39   a) 35, 37   b) 38, 40   c) 37, 38

1. Add.

$\overline{1}\,5$	$\overline{1}\,9$	$\overline{1}\,6$	$\overline{1}\,7$	$\overline{1}\,8$
$+\,1\,5$	$+\,1\,5$	$+\,1\,8$	$+\,1\,7$	$+\,1\,5$

$\overline{3}\,5$	$\overline{3}\,4$	$\overline{3}\,8$	$\overline{3}\,9$	$\overline{3}\,6$
$+\,2\,8$	$+\,2\,9$	$+\,2\,7$	$+\,2\,8$	$+\,2\,7$

$\overline{7}\,5$	$\overline{9}\,4$	$\overline{5}\,7$	$\overline{8}\,9$	$\overline{6}\,6$
$+\,2\,5$	$+\,1\,7$	$+\,3\,8$	$+\,3\,9$	$+\,4\,6$

19 + 15 = 19 + 1 + 14 = __

$\boxed{1 + 14}$

38 + 27 = __ + __ + __ = __

$\boxed{2 + 25}$

89 + 39 = __ + __ + __ = __

$\boxed{1 + 38}$

1. Add.

$$\begin{array}{r} \overline{3}\ 8 \\ +\ 5\ 5 \\ \hline \end{array} \qquad \begin{array}{r} \overline{2}\ 9 \\ +\ 4\ 5 \\ \hline \end{array} \qquad \begin{array}{r} \overline{7}\ 6 \\ +\ 2\ 8 \\ \hline \end{array} \qquad \begin{array}{r} \overline{3}\ 7 \\ +\ 6\ 7 \\ \hline \end{array} \qquad \begin{array}{r} \overline{9}\ 3 \\ +\ 2\ 7 \\ \hline \end{array}$$

$$\begin{array}{r} \overline{2}\ 7 \\ +\ 3\ 8 \\ \hline \end{array} \qquad \begin{array}{r} \overline{3}\ 4 \\ +\ 4\ 7 \\ \hline \end{array} \qquad \begin{array}{r} \overline{6}\ 9 \\ +\ 2\ 7 \\ \hline \end{array} \qquad \begin{array}{r} \overline{3}\ 9 \\ +\ 8\ 2 \\ \hline \end{array} \qquad \begin{array}{r} \overline{7}\ 5 \\ +\ 2\ 7 \\ \hline \end{array}$$

$$\begin{array}{r} \overline{4}\ 5 \\ +\ 4\ 6 \\ \hline \end{array} \qquad \begin{array}{r} \overline{5}\ 8 \\ +\ 5\ 7 \\ \hline \end{array} \qquad \begin{array}{r} \overline{6}\ 5 \\ +\ 6\ 8 \\ \hline \end{array} \qquad \begin{array}{r} \overline{7}\ 3 \\ +\ 7\ 9 \\ \hline \end{array} \qquad \begin{array}{r} \overline{8}\ 6 \\ +\ 8\ 9 \\ \hline \end{array}$$

76 + 28 = 76 + 30 - 2 = __

$\boxed{30 - 2}$

39 + 82 = __ + __ - __ = __

__ __

58 + 57 = __ + __ - __ = __

__ __

1. I added three addends to 5 and got 30. Write the missing numbers to make the equations true.

$$5 + \_\_ + \_\_ + \_\_ = 30$$

$$5 + \_\_ + \_\_ + \_\_ = 30$$

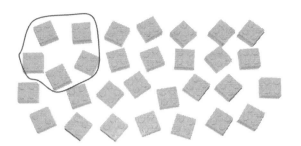

No trouble! I circle 5 bricks and arrange the leftover bricks in any order.

2. My goal was to make 17 cakes. I made double. How many cakes did I make?

Circle your answer.

a) 35   b) 33   c) 34

3. Count shapes. How many:

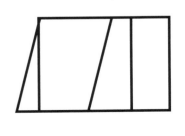

rectangles?
____

circles?
____

1. <u>Find</u> the missing numbers.

<u>Remember:</u> Whole = Part1 + Part2.

😊 - 3 = 47   😊 - 2 = 78   😊 - 8 = 52

😊 = __   😊 = __   😊 = __

? - 4 = 26   ? - 6 = 44   ? - 9 = 81

? = __   ? = __   ? = __

🐭 - 5 = 65   🐵 - 7 = 23   🐼 - 1 = 39

🐭 = __   🐵 = __   🐼 =

2. <u>How many of each</u> shape? <u>Color</u> the boxes for each number on the graph.

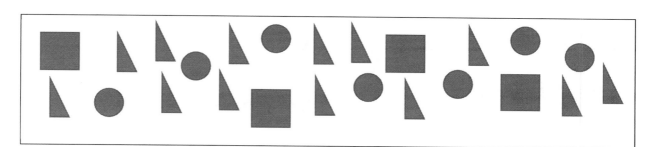

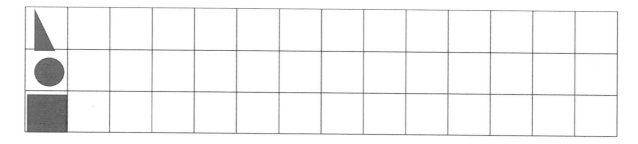

1. <u>Subtract.</u>

$$\begin{array}{r} \overline{4}\ \overline{5} \\ -\ 1\ 7 \\ \hline \end{array} \qquad \begin{array}{r} \overline{3}\ \overline{4} \\ -\ 1\ 8 \\ \hline \end{array} \qquad \begin{array}{r} \overline{8}\ \overline{8} \\ -\ 2\ 9 \\ \hline \end{array} \qquad \begin{array}{r} \overline{5}\ \overline{5} \\ -\ 2\ 7 \\ \hline \end{array} \qquad \begin{array}{r} \overline{7}\ \overline{1} \\ -\ 3\ 5 \\ \hline \end{array}$$

2.   <u>Add</u> or <u>subtract.</u>

400 + 200 = 600   270 + 510 = __   705 + 100 = __

637 + 300 = __   300 + 520 = __   150 + 440 = __

490 – 220 = __   680 – 160 = __   275 – 130 = __

1. <u>Write</u> < or > between the numbers to make the inequality true.

240 _____ 140   28 _____ 89

421 _____ 353   511 _____ 151

642 _____ 624   395 _____ 359

400 _____ 200   153 _____ 687

411 _____ 914   804 _____ 840

2. <u>Write</u> any consecutive numbers.   Consecutive numbers are numbers that follow each other in order.

<u>Write</u> any 3 consecutive numbers.   __, __, __.

<u>Write</u> any 4 consecutive numbers.   __, __, __,

3. I am a two-digit number.

I'm less than 20.   I'm an odd number.

The sum of my digits is 6.

<u>Which number</u> am I?

Answer:

_____.

1. I added two addends to 8 and got 30. <u>Write</u> the missing numbers to make the equations true.

8 + __ + __ = 30

8 + __ + __ = 30

2. I met ⬚7⬚ squirrels on Friday. On Saturday, the number of squirrels I met increased by ⬚6⬚. The number of squirrels I met on Sunday was ⬚8 more⬚ than that of Friday. <u>How many squirrels</u> did I meet in all?

<u>Circle</u> your answer.

a) 35   b) 33   c) 34

3.   <u>Continue</u> the pattern:

99, 88, 77, ____, ____, ____, ____, ____, ____.

4. <u>Write</u> the number from the choice box to make the inequality true.

253 < ____ < 279

a) 251   b) 289   c) 265

1. <u>Write</u> the missing numbers 8, 9, 12, 13, and 26 to make the equation true.

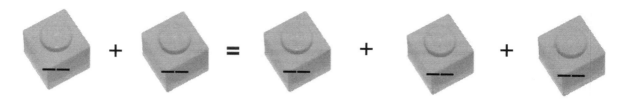

2. <u>Find</u> the route. You can go only right or down at each turn.

Start = 0	+ 6	+ 4	- 8	+ 5
- 4	+ 9	- 5	+ 6	+ 3
- 2	+ 7	- 5	- 9	+ 6
- 2	- 8	- 1	+ 9	- 4
+ 7	+ 8	+ 2	- 3	Finish = 15

3. <u>Write</u> the missing numbers 9, 10, 12, 13, and 18 to make the equation true.

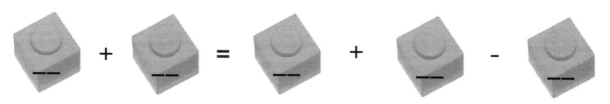

1. <u>Subtract.</u>   Score: ___/15   Time: __ : __

$$\begin{array}{r} 2\ 4 \\ -\ 1\ 6 \\ \hline \end{array} \quad \begin{array}{r} 3\ 3 \\ -\ 1\ 5 \\ \hline \end{array} \quad \begin{array}{r} 8\ 1 \\ -\ 4\ 8 \\ \hline \end{array} \quad \begin{array}{r} 5\ 2 \\ -\ 3\ 7 \\ \hline \end{array} \quad \begin{array}{r} 7\ 5 \\ -\ 2\ 8 \\ \hline \end{array}$$

$$\begin{array}{r} 4\ 2 \\ -\ 2\ 8 \\ \hline \end{array} \quad \begin{array}{r} 5\ 3 \\ -\ 2\ 9 \\ \hline \end{array} \quad \begin{array}{r} 6\ 1 \\ -\ 2\ 7 \\ \hline \end{array} \quad \begin{array}{r} 9\ 4 \\ -\ 2\ 8 \\ \hline \end{array} \quad \begin{array}{r} 7\ 5 \\ -\ 2\ 7 \\ \hline \end{array}$$

$$\begin{array}{r} 7\ 1 \\ -\ 3\ 5 \\ \hline \end{array} \quad \begin{array}{r} 9\ 3 \\ -\ 3\ 7 \\ \hline \end{array} \quad \begin{array}{r} 7\ 2 \\ -\ 3\ 8 \\ \hline \end{array} \quad \begin{array}{r} 6\ 4 \\ -\ 3\ 9 \\ \hline \end{array} \quad \begin{array}{r} 6\ 2 \\ -\ 3\ 6 \\ \hline \end{array}$$

43 - 16 = 43 - 20 + 4 = __

61 - 27 = __ - __ + __ = __

72 - 38 = __ - __ + __ = __

1. Circle the correct answer.

I have a series of numbers: 2, 7, 9, 14, 16, 21, 19, 24, __

What is the next number?

   a) 20   b) 22   c) 29

2. I have some numbers and signs: 15, 5, 10, +, -.

Write the equation that equals one of the answer choices. Circle the correct answer.

_____

   a) 0   b) 30   c) 5

I have some numbers and signs: 27, 5, 12, +, -.

Write the equation that equals one of the answer choices. Circle the correct answer.

_____

   a) 44   b) 31   c) 34

3. Circle an even number to make the statements true.

$18 < \_\_\_ < 34$ a) 12   b) 8   c) 25   d) 32

$64 < \_\_\_ < 80$ a) 78   b) 102   c) 48   d) 56

1. <u>Subtract.</u>

$$\begin{array}{r} \bar{7}\,\bar{1} \\ -\ 4\ 9 \\ \hline \end{array} \qquad \begin{array}{r} \bar{5}\,\bar{3} \\ -\ 3\ 5 \\ \hline \end{array} \qquad \begin{array}{r} \bar{6}\,\bar{0} \\ -\ 1\ 7 \\ \hline \end{array} \qquad \begin{array}{r} \bar{4}\,\bar{2} \\ -\ 2\ 4 \\ \hline \end{array} \qquad \begin{array}{r} \bar{9}\,\bar{7} \\ -\ 5\ 8 \\ \hline \end{array}$$

2. I added two addends to 6 and got 31. <u>Write</u> the missing numbers to make the equations true.

6 + __ + __ = 31

6 + __ + __ = 31

3. I read ⑨ pages on Friday. On Saturday, I read ⑫ pages. The number of pages I read on Sunday was ⑦ less than that of Friday and Saturday. <u>How many pages</u> did I read in all? <u>Circle</u> the correct answer.

a) 31   b) 34   c) 35

4. <u>Find</u> the missing numbers.

? + 200 = 700   ? + 400 = 900   ? + 100 = 700

? = ___   ? = ___   ? = ___

1. <u>Add</u>.

$$\begin{array}{r} \overline{2}\ 5 \\ +\ 3\ 9 \\ \hline \end{array}$$
$$\begin{array}{r} \overline{6}\ 4 \\ +\ 2\ 8 \\ \hline \end{array}$$
$$\begin{array}{r} \overline{8}\ 3 \\ +\ 1\ 7 \\ \hline \end{array}$$
$$\begin{array}{r} \overline{3}\ 7 \\ +\ 5\ 4 \\ \hline \end{array}$$
$$\begin{array}{r} \overline{7}\ 5 \\ +\ 1\ 8 \\ \hline \end{array}$$

2.

I wanted to use 18 blocks to build a tower but I used double. How many blocks did I use?

Answer: _____

3. <u>Find</u> the missing even consecutive numbers. Consecutive numbers are numbers that follow each other in order. <u>Circle</u> the correct answer.

__, 28   a) 27   b) 26   c) 24

16, __, __   a) 12, 14   b) 18, 20   c) 17, 18

__, __, 32, __   a) 30, 31, 34   b) 28, 30, 33   c) 28, 30, 34

__, __, 50   a) 46, 48   b) 48, 49   c) 40, 44

1. Subtract.

| $\begin{array}{r} \bar{5}\,\bar{1} \\ -\ 2\ 4 \end{array}$ | $\begin{array}{r} \bar{7}\,\bar{3} \\ -\ 4\ 7 \end{array}$ | $\begin{array}{r} \bar{4}\,\bar{0} \\ -\ 1\ 5 \end{array}$ | $\begin{array}{r} \bar{8}\,\bar{2} \\ -\ 5\ 3 \end{array}$ | $\begin{array}{r} \bar{6}\,\bar{7} \\ -\ 3\ 9 \end{array}$ |

2. I have some numbers and signs:

14, 7, 21, +, -.

Write the equation that equals one of the answer choices. Circle the correct answer.

_____

a) 29   b) 24   c) 14

3. What is the value of the 5 in each of these numbers? Circle the correct answer.

3591   a) Thousands   b) Hundreds   b) Tens   c) Ones

2658   a) Thousands   b) Hundreds   b) Tens   c) Ones

5902   a) Thousands   b) Hundreds   b) Tens   c) Ones

3665   a) Thousands   b) Hundreds   b) Tens   c) Ones

1. <u>Find</u> the missing numbers.

? - 200 = 300   ? - 300 = 600   ? - 100 = 700

? = ___   ? = ___   ? = ___

2. <u>Write and put</u> the numbers in order from the largest to the smallest.

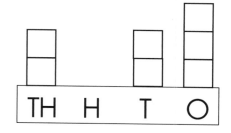

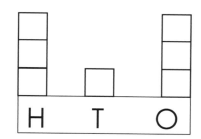   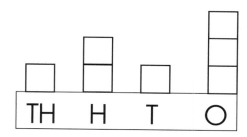

_____   _____   _____

3. I encountered 15 monsters yesterday. 8 of them I destroyed. Today I encountered 21 monsters. 13 of them I destroyed. <u>How many monsters</u> couldn't I destroy?

Answer: _____.

1. <u>Skip</u> <u>count</u> by 10's to 790.

300 310 320 __ __ __ __ __ __ __

__ __ __ __ __ __ __ __ __ __

__ __ __ __ __ __ __ __ __ __

__ __ __ __ __ __ __ __ __ __

__ __ __ __ __ __ __ __ __ 790

2. <u>Find</u> the missing numbers.

☺ + 125 = 675   ☺ + 375 = 595   ☺ + 425 = 575

☺ = ___   ☺ = ___   ☺ = ___

3. <u>Write</u> these numbers in the correct section.

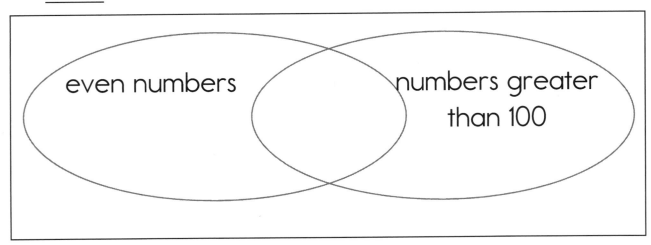

even numbers   numbers greater
                         than 100

112, 64, 86, 124, 135, 76, 13, 192, 50, 27, 45, 286, 341, 204

1. Add.

$$\overline{6}\ 6 \qquad \overline{8}\ 8 \qquad \overline{3}\ 3 \qquad \overline{5}\ 5 \qquad \overline{7}\ 7$$
$$+\ 1\ 5 \qquad +\ 2\ 7 \qquad +\ 1\ 9 \qquad +\ 2\ 8 \qquad +\ 1\ 6$$

2. Find the missing numbers.

☺ - 125 = 673   ☺ - 314 = 254   ☺ - 423 = 521

☺ = ___   ☺ = ___   ☺ = ___

3. Circle the right answer.

A: 45 – 29   a) A is greater than B
B: 23 + 19   b) A is less than B
                          c) A is equal to B

A: 25 + 47 - 36   a) A is greater than B
B: 70 – 48 + 14   b) A is less than B
                          c) A is equal to B

A: 54 – 19   a) A is greater than B
B: 82 – 65   b) A is less than B
                          c) A is equal to B

1. <u>Continue</u> the pattern:

98, 94, 88, _____, _____, _____, _____, _____, _____.

2. <u>Circle</u> the right answer.

A: 41 - 25 + 19   a) A is greater than B
B: 41 + 19 - 25   b) A is less than B
                              c) A is equal to B

A: 91 – 67   a) A is greater than B
B: 78 – 39   b) A is less than B
                              c) A is equal to B

3. <u>Find out</u> <u>what number</u> is hiding.

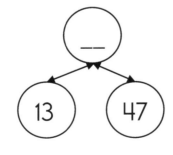
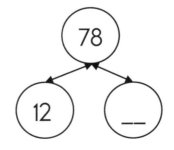
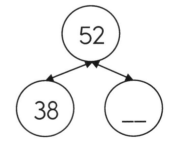

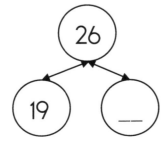
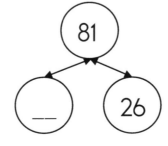
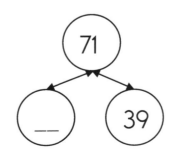

1. <u>Subtract.</u>   Score: ___/15   Time: __ : __

```
  2 4        6 7        9 3        5 5        7 8
- 1 1      - 3 5      - 6 1      - 2 4      - 5 7
```

```
  3 0        3 0        5 0        9 0        4 0
- 1 8      - 2 1      - 3 6      - 4 4      - 1 8
```

```
  7 0        5 0        2 0        8 0        6 0
- 5 6      - 3 4      - 1 2      - 4 5      - 2 9
```

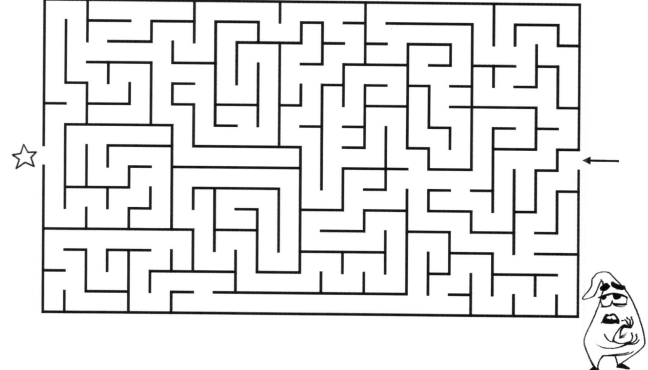

1. I'm building a solid wall of rocks: the two rocks next to each other are added to get the number up above. Fill in the missing numbers.

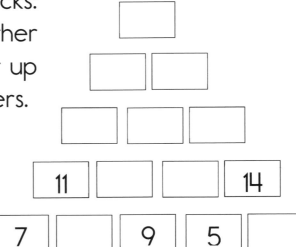

2. Subtract.

600 - 300 =_____   900-600= ____   800-500= ____

700 - 600 = ____   700-300= ____   400-300= ____

900 - 400 = ____   800-200= ____   300-200= ____

800 - 400 = ____   600-200= ____   900-100= ____

700 - 500 = ____   400-200= ____   800-300= ____

3. Compare and find out how many more or less the numbers are different by.

100 > 50 by 50   30 < 60 by ___

70 > 10 by ___   40 < 90 by ___

60 > 20 by ___   50 < 70 by ___

Hint: Ones under ones, tens under tens, hundreds under hundreds;
Subtract ones, then tens, then hundreds.

300 - 129

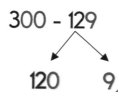

120   9

Decompose 129.
129 is 120+9.

300 – 129 =
300-120-9=180-9=171
or 300 – 129 =
300-130+1=170+1=171.

hundreds   tens   ones

3   0   0
-      1   2   9
___   ___   ___

Step 1: To subtract in columns, I need one row above 300.

Step 2: Borrow 1 ten of the 30 tens. Write 10 ones above 0 ones. Write 29 above 30 tens: 30-1=29.

Step 3: Cross out 0 ones and 30 tens.

Step 4: Subtract 9 ones from 10 ones: 10-9=1.

H   T   O
2   9   10
3̶   0̶   0̶
- 1   2   9
___   ___   ___

Step 5: Subtract 2 tens from 9 tens: 9-2=7.

Step 6: Subtract 1 hundred from 2 hundred: 2-1=1.

H   T   O
2   9   10
3̶   0̶   0̶
- 1   2   9
___   ___   ___
1   7   1

1. <u>Subtract.</u>   Score: ___/12   Time: __ : __

$$
\begin{array}{r} 8\ \ 9\ \ 10 \\ \cancel{9}\ \ \cancel{0}\ \ \cancel{0} \\ -\ 3\ \ 2\ \ 5 \\ \hline \end{array}
\qquad
\begin{array}{r} 6\ \ 9\ \ 10 \\ \cancel{7}\ \ \cancel{0}\ \ \cancel{0} \\ -\ 1\ \ 2\ \ 5 \\ \hline \end{array}
\qquad
\begin{array}{r} 7\ \ 9\ \ 10 \\ \cancel{8}\ \ \cancel{0}\ \ \cancel{0} \\ -\ 2\ \ 2\ \ 5 \\ \hline \end{array}
\qquad
\begin{array}{r} 5\ \ 9\ \ 10 \\ \cancel{6}\ \ \cancel{0}\ \ \cancel{0} \\ -\ 3\ \ 8\ \ 1 \\ \hline \end{array}
$$

$$
\begin{array}{r} \overline{5}\ \ \overline{0}\ \ \overline{0} \\ -\ 2\ \ 8\ \ 4 \\ \hline \end{array}
\qquad
\begin{array}{r} \overline{8}\ \ \overline{0}\ \ \overline{0} \\ -\ 6\ \ 1\ \ 7 \\ \hline \end{array}
\qquad
\begin{array}{r} \overline{9}\ \ \overline{0}\ \ \overline{0} \\ -\ 7\ \ 3\ \ 8 \\ \hline \end{array}
\qquad
\begin{array}{r} \overline{3}\ \ \overline{0}\ \ \overline{0} \\ -\ 1\ \ 9\ \ 2 \\ \hline \end{array}
$$

$$
\begin{array}{r} \overline{7}\ \ \overline{0}\ \ \overline{0} \\ -\ 4\ \ 7\ \ 2 \\ \hline \end{array}
\qquad
\begin{array}{r} \overline{4}\ \ \overline{0}\ \ \overline{0} \\ -\ 1\ \ 6\ \ 8 \\ \hline \end{array}
\qquad
\begin{array}{r} \overline{8}\ \ \overline{0}\ \ \overline{0} \\ -\ 4\ \ 9\ \ 5 \\ \hline \end{array}
\qquad
\begin{array}{r} \overline{9}\ \ \overline{0}\ \ \overline{0} \\ -\ 6\ \ 3\ \ 1 \\ \hline \end{array}
$$

2. I used 41 rocks yesterday. 13 of them hit the target. Today I used 34 rocks. 19 of them hit the target. <u>How many more or less rocks</u> hit the target yesterday?

Answer: _____.

1. <u>Subtract.</u>   Score: ___/12   Time: __ : __

```
  7 0 0        3 0 0        5 0 0        4 0 0
- 1 6 7      - 1 8 6      - 2 7 1      - 2 8 9
```

```
  6 0 0        8 0 0        9 0 0        3 0 0
- 3 2 7      - 4 1 6      - 5 4 5      - 1 2 4
```

```
  4 0 0        5 0 0        6 0 0        7 0 0
- 1 5 8      - 3 2 1      - 5 1 7      - 3 9 9
```

2. My brother and I have 65 dollars altogether. If I have 29 dollars more, <u>how many dollars</u> does he have? <u>Circle</u> the correct answer.

a) 21   b) 19   c) 18

1. <u>Arrange</u> the numbers from the least to the greatest. The first one is done for you.

34	87	25	96	54	13	76	102	94	37	65	41	59
13	__	__	__	__	__	__	__	__	__	__	__	__

2. <u>Add</u> or <u>subtract</u>.

712 + 26 = __   521 + 73 = __   918 + 31 = __

624 + 25 = __   346 + 52 = __   253 + 36 = __

433 – 33 = __   862 – 41 = __   528 – 25 = __

848 – 36 = __   268 – 51 = __   729 – 27 = __

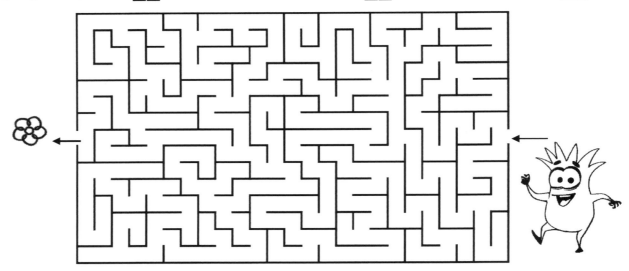

3. <u>Subtract</u>. Hint: 710 – 160 = 710 – 200 + 40 = ___

710 - 160 = __   820 - 470 = __   320 - 170 = __

540 - 490 = __   640 - 390 = __   960 - 280 = __

650 - 380 = __   430 - 160 = __   830 - 790 = __

1. <u>Skip count</u> by 10's to 590.

100   110   120   __   __   __   __   __   __   __

__   __   __   __   __   __   __   __   __   __

__   __   __   __   __   __   __   __   __   __

__   __   __   __   __   __   __   __   __   __

__   __   __   __   __   __   __   __   __   590

2. <u>Circle</u> the correct answer.

A: 75 - 39 + 26   a) A is greater than B

B: 67 + 25 - 14   b) A is less than B

                                            c) A is equal to B

3. <u>Subtract.</u>

```
   5 0 0        9 0 0        7 0 0        6 0 0
 - 2 4 8      - 3 7 1      - 5 0 2      - 3 4 6
```

4. <u>Circle</u> the correct answer.

__ 6 + 5 7 = 93

    a) 4   b) 3   c) 2

1. Subtract.

800 - 250 = __   1000 – 350 = __

900 - 450 = __   1000 – 750 = __

700 - 550 = __   500 – 150 = __

600 – 350 = __   1000 – 550 = __

400 – 150 = __   800 – 450 = __

900 – 650 = __   700 – 350 = __

2. Fill in the missing numbers to make the equations true.

__ + __ + __ = 45

__ + __ + __ = 39

__ + __ + __ = 32

1. <u>Round</u> each number to the nearest 10. <u>Look</u> at the next digit to the right. If it is 0, 1, 2, 3, or 4 then ROUND DOWN, if it is 5, 6, 7, 8, 9 then, ROUND UP. The first one is done for you.

24<u>3</u> 240   47<u>4</u> ____   21<u>6</u> ____   59<u>1</u> ____

82<u>7</u> ____   37<u>9</u> ____   74<u>2</u> ___   65<u>5</u> ____

2. <u>Round</u> each number to the nearest 100. <u>Look</u> at the next digit to the right. If it is 0, 1, 2, 3, or 4 then, ROUND DOWN, if it is 5, 6, 7, 8, 9 then, ROUND UP. The first one is done for you.

2<u>3</u>5 200   4<u>4</u>9 ____   1<u>6</u>7 ____   5<u>1</u>8 ____

8<u>7</u>3 ____   3<u>9</u>5 ____   7<u>2</u>0 ____   6<u>5</u>7 ____

3. <u>Circle</u> the right answer.

__ 8 + 4 4 = 82   a) 5   b) 3   c) 6

5 3 + 3 __ = 91   a) 7   b) 9   c) 8

3 8 + 2 7 = __ 5   a) 8   b) 5   c) 6

1. Venn Diagram: helps you sort things according to their different features.

I have many books. 10 of them are fantasy blocks. 8 of them are adventure books. 6 of them are fantasy and adventure books. 7 of them are history books. How many books are there? Fill in the diagram.

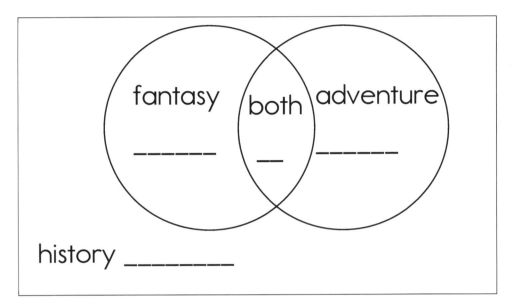

history _____

Answer: _____

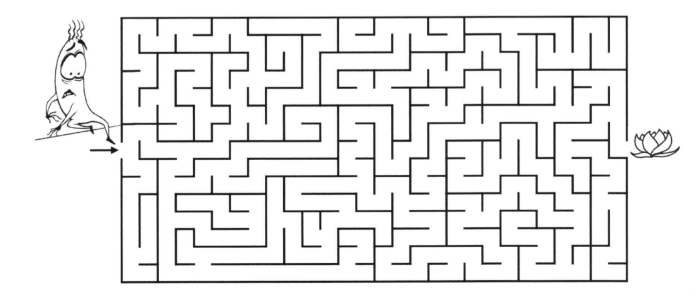

Hint: Ones under ones, tens under tens, hundreds under hundreds;
Subtract ones, then tens, then hundreds.

$345 - 178$

120   9

Decompose 178.
178 is 145+33.

$345 - 178 =$

$345-145-33=200-33=167$

or $345 - 178 =$

$345-200+22=145+22=167.$

	hundreds	tens	ones
	3	4	5
-	1	7	8
	—	—	—

Step 1: To subtract in columns, I need one row above 345.

Step 2: Borrow 1 ten of the 4 tens. Write 15 ones above 5 ones. Write 3 above 4 tens: 4-1=3.

Step 3: Cross out 5 ones and 4 tens.

Step 4: Subtract 8 ones from 15 ones: 15-8=7.

H	T	O
3	3	15
3	4	5
- 1	7	8

Step 5: Borrow 1 hundred of the 3 hundreds. Write 13 tens above 4 tens. Subtract tens: 13-7=7.

Step 6: Subtract hundreds: 2-1=1.

H	T	O
2	13	15
3	4	5
- 1	7	8
1	7	7

1. Subtract.

Score: ___/12   Time: __ : __

```
  6 11 14
  7  1  4         3 2 8         5 3 3         4 2 5
- 1  9  6       - 1 3 9       - 2 5 5       - 2 3 6
  5  2  8
```

```
  6 1 5         8 2 2         9 4 1         3 6 3
- 3 4 6       - 4 6 4       - 5 7 2       - 1 9 5
```

```
  4 4 2         5 7 4         6 9 1         7 7 7
- 1 6 3       - 3 8 7       - 5 9 2       - 4 8 8
```

2. Choose any of the three digits to make the total as close as possible to 500. Circle the correct answer.

197 + _____ = 500

a) 1, 9, 8   b) 2, 5, 6   c) 0, 3, 3

1. <u>Fill in</u> the missing numbers. 1 letter is 1 digit (tens or ones).

A6 + 3B = 75   4C + D2 = 91   15E + 1HF = G00

_ 6 + 3 _ = 75   4 _ + _ 2 = 91   15 _+1 _ 6 = _ 00

A6 + 4B = 120   3C + D9 = 86   6E + F9 = G00

_ 6 + 4 _ = 120   3 _ + _ 9 = 86   6 _ + _ 9 = _ 00

2. <u>Answer</u> the questions.

<u>Find</u> the missing 1 even consecutive number. __, 28.

<u>Find</u> the missing 2 odd consecutive numbers. 15, __,__.

<u>Find</u> the missing 2 even consecutive numbers. __,__,32

3. <u>Subtract</u>. <u>Hint:</u> 325 – 175 = 325 – 125 – 50 = 200 – 50 = 150.

950 - 250 = __   750 - 30 = __   400 - 350 = __

675 - 225 = __   950 - 425 = __   625 - 375 = __

1. <u>Arrange</u> the numbers from the least to the greatest.

44	38	100	90	52	95	77	21	65	37	89	46	11
11	__	__	__	__	__	__	__	__	__	__	__	__

2. <u>Arrange</u> the numbers from the greatest to the least.

36	97	18	29	33	80	15	95	84	63	42	51	77
97	__	__	__	__	__	__	__	__	__	__	__	__

3. <u>Subtract.</u>   Score: ___/12   Time: __ : __

```
   4 7 1        5 3 7        8 2 4        9 3 1
 - 2 9 2      - 3 3 8      - 4 5 6      - 3 5 2
 _____      _____      _____      _____


   5 0 1        4 7 0        3 0 5        6 3 0
 - 3 3 7      - 1 3 9      - 1 2 7      - 4 8 2
 _____      _____      _____      _____


   3 3 3        5 5 5        2 2 2        6 6 6
 - 1 4 8      - 2 9 6      - 1 3 4      - 3 7 9
 _____      _____      _____      _____
```

1. <u>Find</u> the missing numbers.

100 - ☺ = 7   100 - ☺ = 8   100 – ☺ = 2

☺ = __   ☺ = __   ☺ = __

100 - ? = 6   100 - ? = 4   100 - ? = 1

? = __   ? = __   ? = __

100 - ☺ = 5   100 - ☺ = 3   100 - ☺ = 9

☺ = __   ☺ = __   ☺ = __

2. <u>Fill in</u> the missing numbers to make the equations true.

    | __ + __ + __ = 39

    | __ + __ + __ = 31

    | __ + __ + __ = 41

3. <u>Continue</u> a series of numbers.

5, 10, 15, __ __, __ __, __ __, __ __ , __ __ , __ __, __ __.

1. Tallying: tally marks help you keep track of numbers in groups of five.

I have two brothers and two sisters. This graph shows the number of dollars collected by each of us.

How many dollars do the boys have?

_____

How many dollars do Oliver and James have altogether?

_____

How many more dollars does Emma have than Evelyn?

_____

What is the total number of dollars?

_____

	Dollars
I, Jack	ЖTT ЖTT ЖTT
Oliver	ЖTT ЖTT ЖTT
James	ЖTT IIII
Emma	ЖTT ЖTT IIII
Evelyn	ЖTT III

2. Continue a series of numbers.

2, 8, 5, 11, 8, _____, _____, _____, _____, _____, _____.

4, 9, 15, 22, 30, _____, _____, _____, _____, _____, _____.

1. <u>Use</u> < or > to make these statements true.

46 __ 75 __ 26   246 __ 169 __ 762

13 __ 96 __ 132   35 __ 12 __ 86

75 __ 21 __ 59   70 __ 24 __ 65

164 __ 200 __ 97   416 __ 235__ 102

2. <u>Write</u> these numbers in order, from the smallest to the largest.

637, 120, 371, 97, 481, 56, 972, 40

_____

111, 842, 37, 890, 75, 614, 89, 201

_____

3. <u>Add.</u>

```
    227          409          840          712
+   131      +   350      +   125      +   226
─────────    ─────────    ─────────    ─────────
```

1. <u>Round</u> each number to the nearest 10.

51<u>5</u> ____   90<u>1</u> ____   36<u>8</u> ____   63<u>4</u>_ ____

86<u>0</u>____   51<u>7</u> ____   28<u>3</u> ___   91<u>8</u> _____

2. <u>Round</u> each number to the nearest 100.

7<u>5</u>6 _____   1<u>9</u>3 _____   4<u>3</u>8 _____   7<u>7</u>0_____

9<u>0</u>5_____   2<u>6</u>6 _____   4<u>1</u>7 _____   8<u>4</u>9____

3. <u>Circle</u> the correct answer.

A: 51 - 26 + 14   a) A is greater than B

B: 83 - 38 - 16   b) A is less than B

c) A is equal to B

4. <u>Add.</u>

$$
\begin{array}{r} 745 \\ +\ \ 212 \\ \hline \end{array}
\qquad
\begin{array}{r} 852 \\ +\ \ 435 \\ \hline \end{array}
\qquad
\begin{array}{r} 577 \\ +\ \ 111 \\ \hline \end{array}
\qquad
\begin{array}{r} 439 \\ +\ \ 440 \\ \hline \end{array}
$$

1. <u>Subtract.</u>

750 - 150 = ___   300 - 150 = ___   550 - 450 = ___

600 - 350 = ___   900 - 250 = ___   400 – 250 = ___

 I like both ways: 800 - 450 = 800 – 400 – 50 or 800 – 500 + 50. The answer is 350.

2. The sum of 2 even numbers is 30 and their difference is 6. <u>What</u> are these even numbers?

Answer: _____.

Let's make subtraction easy and fun!

```
 H  T  O
 3  0  0
-1  5  5
___ ___ ___
```

Step 1: To subtract from 3 hundreds in columns, I need to subtract 1 from both numbers.

```
 H  T  O          H  T  O
 3  0  0  -1      2  9  9
-1  5  5  -1  →  -1  5  4
 1  7  7          1  4  5
```

Step 2: Subtract 4 ones from 9 ones: 9-4=5.

Step 2: Subtract 5 tens from 9 tens: 9-5=4.

Step 2: Subtract 1 hundred from 2 hundreds: 2-1=1.

1. Subtract.

```
 6 0 0 -1      _ _ _        5 0 0 -1      _ _ _
-3 9 2 -1    - _ _ _      -2 4 6 -1    - _ _ _
```

2. Subtract.

650 - 350 = __   400 - 150 = __   800 - 750 = __

1. <u>Subtract.</u>　　　　Score: ___/12　　　Time: __ : __

```
   ‾ ‾ ‾        ‾ ‾ ‾        ‾ ‾ ‾        ‾ ‾ ‾
   5 2 7        5 2 1        6 2 5        8 2 7
 - 1 4 8      - 2 4 7      - 3 4 9      - 4 4 9
```

```
   ‾ ‾ ‾        ‾ ‾ ‾        ‾ ‾ ‾        ‾ ‾ ‾
   5 1 0        6 1 0        9 4 0        5 2 0
 - 2 7 6      - 3 3 4      - 5 9 4      - 1 8 3
```

```
   ‾ ‾ ‾        ‾ ‾ ‾        ‾ ‾ ‾        ‾ ‾ ‾
   6 0 0        7 0 0        4 0 0        3 0 0
 - 3 5 4      - 3 2 7      - 2 9 9      - 2 4 2
```

2. <u>Subtract.</u>

```
   9 0 0 ⁻¹        _ _ _        7 0 0 ⁻¹        _ _ _
 - 6 3 7 ⁻¹      - _ _ _      - 3 6 9 ⁻¹      - _ _ _
```

345 + 198

5   193

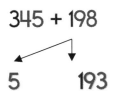

Decompose 198. 198 is 5+193.

345+5+193=350+193=543

345+200-2=545-2=543

```
  H  T  O
  3  4  5
+ 1  9  8
  _  _  _
```

Step 1: I need one more row above 345.

Step 2: Add ones: 5+8=13.

```
  H  T  O
  ‾  ‾
  3  4  5
+ 1  9  8
  _  _  _
```

Write the 3 in one's place. Carry 1 ten with the other tens. Write the 1 above 4 in ten's place.

```
  H  T  O
     1
  ‾
  3  4  5
+ 1  9  8
  _  _  3
```

Step 3: Add tens: 1+4+9=14 Write the 4 in ten's place. Carry 1 hundred with the other hundreds. Write the 1 above 3 in hundred's place.

Step 4: Add hundreds: 1+3+1=5.

```
  H  T  O
  1  1
  3  4  5
+ 1  9  8
  5  4  3
```

1. Add.

```
    ‾
  5 2 4
+ 2 4 8
```

```
    ‾
  2 3 7
+ 3 4 3
```

```
  ‾ ‾
  4 7 2
+ 2 3 8
```

```
  ‾ ‾
  6 1 8
+ 1 9 5
```

1. Add or subtract.

Count up.

Hint: 100 – 95 = 100 – 100 + 5. 72 + 18 = 72 + 20 – 2.

100 – 95 = __	60 – 52 = __	20 – 18 = __
80 – 74 = __	40 – 39 = __	70 – 61 = __
50 – 46 = __	30 – 23 = __	90 – 87 = __
72 + 18 = __	17 + 43 = __	46 + 24 = __
51 + 39 = __	28 + 22 = __	63 + 17 = __
24 + 56 = __	39 + 21 = __	75 + 15 = __

2. Add.

$$\begin{array}{r} 2\ 3\ 4 \\ +\ 3\ 6\ 7 \\ \hline \end{array} \qquad \begin{array}{r} 4\ 8\ 7 \\ +\ 1\ 3\ 7 \\ \hline \end{array} \qquad \begin{array}{r} 3\ 5\ 2 \\ +\ 3\ 6\ 9 \\ \hline \end{array} \qquad \begin{array}{r} 1\ 4\ 6 \\ +\ 4\ 3\ 9 \\ \hline \end{array}$$

3. Subtract.

$$\begin{array}{r} 9\ 0\ 0 \\ -\ 4\ 6\ 1 \\ \hline \end{array} \qquad \begin{array}{r} 9\ 0\ 0 \\ -\ 5\ 2\ 8 \\ \hline \end{array} \qquad \begin{array}{r} 9\ 0\ 0 \\ -\ 6\ 7\ 3 \\ \hline \end{array} \qquad \begin{array}{r} 9\ 0\ 0 \\ -\ 8\ 0\ 2 \\ \hline \end{array}$$

1. Add.

480 + 310 = ___   250 + 290 = ___

150 + 180 = ___   270 + 220 = ___

450 + 370 = ___   650 + 290 = ___

2. Find the missing numbers.

☺ – 200 = 300   ☺ = ___

☺ – 400 = 600   ☺ = ___

☺ – 100 = 700   ☺ = ___

3. Continue a series of numbers.

2, 4, 8, 14, _____, _____, _____, _____, _____, _____.

4, 5, 7, 10, _____, _____, _____, _____, _____, _____.

4. Fill in the missing numbers.

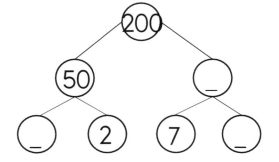
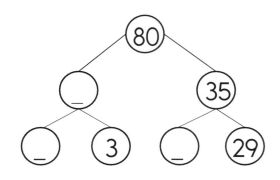

1. <u>Circle</u> the correct answer.

A   73 – 16 - 25

B   83 – 16 - 25

a) A is greater than B

b) A is less than B

c) A is equal to B

2. <u>Arrange</u> the numbers from the least to the greatest.

46	27	95	31	49	82	76	15	58	93	108	64	57
15	__	__	__	__	__	__	__	__	__	__	__	__

3. <u>Add</u> or <u>subtract</u>.

I LOVE mental math!

70 – 36 = 70 – 30 – 6 = 40 – 6 = 34.

64 + 18 = 64 + 6 + 12 = 70 + 12 = 82.

I HATE mental math!

100 – 75 = __   100 – 92 = __   100 – 88 = __

80 – 44 = __   80 – 69 = __   80 – 51 = __

50 – 16 = __   50 – 33 = __   50 – 27 = __

62 +38 = __   87 + 13 = __   46 + 54 = __

31 + 69 = __   28 + 72 = __   53 + 47 = __

44 + 56 = __   99 + 1 = __   75 + 25 = __

1. Subtract. The first one is done for you.

Strategy: 164 - 70 = 164 – 100 + 30 = 64 + 30 = 94.☺.

141 – 50 = 41 + 50 = 91

137 – 80 = _____

129 – 40 = _____

105 - 96 = _____

104 - 96 = _____

101 - 92 = _____

150 - 65 = _____   161 - 92 = _____

154 - 99 = _____   172 - 93 = _____

185 - 98 = _____   153 - 97 = _____

2. Count the squares below to find the perimeter of the whole square and the perimeter of the shaded shape.

Perimeter is the distance around the shape. Hint: To find the perimeter of a rectangle, you need to add the lengths of the rectangle's four sides.

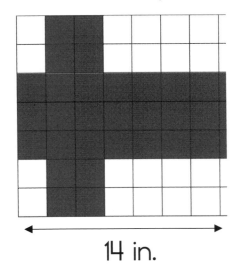

14 in.

Answer: _____.

2nd Grade Math Workbook Addition and Subtraction

1. <u>Add.</u>   Score: ___/8   Time: __ : __

$$\begin{array}{r} \bar{9}\;\bar{2}\;5 \\ +\;3\;8\;6 \\ \hline \end{array}$$
$$\begin{array}{r} \bar{6}\;\bar{9}\;3 \\ +\;1\;4\;7 \\ \hline \end{array}$$
$$\begin{array}{r} \bar{8}\;\bar{6}\;3 \\ +\;3\;5\;8 \\ \hline \end{array}$$
$$\begin{array}{r} \bar{7}\;\bar{9}\;6 \\ +\;2\;4\;6 \\ \hline \end{array}$$

$$\begin{array}{r} \bar{6}\;\bar{4}\;5 \\ +\;2\;7\;5 \\ \hline \end{array}$$
$$\begin{array}{r} \bar{5}\;\bar{3}\;5 \\ +\;1\;9\;8 \\ \hline \end{array}$$
$$\begin{array}{r} \bar{7}\;\bar{2}\;4 \\ +\;5\;8\;8 \\ \hline \end{array}$$
$$\begin{array}{r} \bar{6}\;\bar{7}\;5 \\ +\;4\;3\;6 \\ \hline \end{array}$$

2. Choose any of the three digits to make the total as close as possible to 650. <u>Circle</u> the correct answer.

345 + _____ = 650

a) 3, 5, 5   b) 2, 0, 5   c) 3, 5, 0

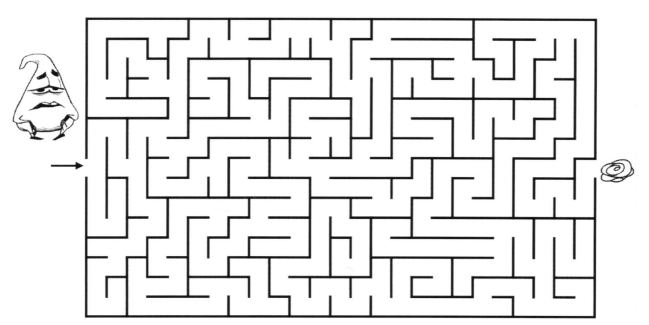

© 2020 Home Run Press, LLC

1. I have several shapes. The perimeter of each is $\boxed{41}$ feet. In each picture one of the measurements has disappeared. <u>Write</u> the length that should be on the missing side.

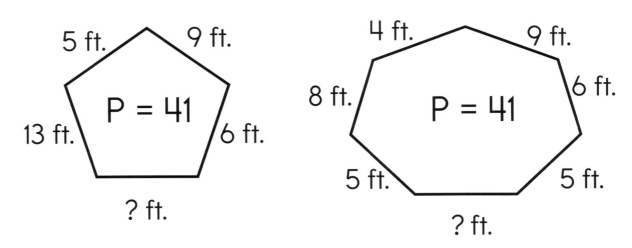

2. Last time I used a ton of blocks. You can write the number written as the largest possible number that you can make by using the digits 0, 1, 3. <u>How many blocks</u> did I use?

Answer: _____.

3. <u>Fill in</u> the missing "+", "-", or "=" to make the equations true. You can use the sign ("+", "-", or "=") more than once.

6 ____ 8 ____ 10 ____ 12   5 ____ 9 ____ 7 ____ 7

11 ____ 5 ____ 4 ____ 10   15 ____ 6 ____ 3 ____ 12

16 ____ 7 ____ 19 ____ 10   22 ____ 9 ____ 7 ____ 24

1. <u>Find</u> the missing even consecutive numbers. <u>Circle</u> the correct answer.

20, __, __.	A) 21, 22	B) 23, 25	C) 22, 24
__, __, 44.	A) 38, 36	B) 38, 40	C) 40, 42
__, 68, __.	A) 70, 72	B) 66, 70	C) 66, 72

2. <u>Add</u>.

$120 + 330 =$ ___ $350 + 490 =$ ___ $450 + 170 =$ ___

$160 + 630 =$ ___ $750 + 160 =$ ___ $350 + 260 =$ ___

$540 + 240 =$ ___ $850 + 80 =$ ___ $350 + 380 =$ ___

3. <u>Find</u> the missing numbers.

$? - 125 = 672$ $? - 375 = 225$ $? - 425 = 575$

$? =$ ____ $? =$ ____ $? =$ ____

4. <u>Write</u> the number.

<u>Which value</u> is equal to 20 tens?   _____

<u>Which value</u> is equal to 52 hundreds?   _____

1. <u>Find</u> the missing addend.

Hint: 40 − 13 = 40 − 10 − 3 = 40 − 13 = 40 − 20 + 7 = 27

☺ + 13 = 40   ☺ + 42 = 80   ☺ + 28 = 70

☺ = ___   ☺ = ___   ☺ = ___

? + 84 = 100   ? + 56 = 70   ? + 39 = 50

? = ___   ? = ___   ? = ___

☺ + 75 = 90   ☺ + 97 = 100   ☺ + 61 = 80

☺ = ___   ☺ = ___   ☺ = ___

2. I spent 91 arrows to destroy the spiders. My brother used 23 arrows less than I used. If my sister used 48 arrows less than I used, <u>how many arrows</u> did we use altogether? <u>Circle</u> the correct answer.

a) 200   b) 196   c) 202

3. <u>Subtract</u>.

$$\begin{array}{r} 8\ 0\ 0 \\ -\ 6\ 2\ 9 \\ \hline \end{array} \qquad \begin{array}{r} 5\ 0\ 0 \\ -\ 2\ 4\ 6 \\ \hline \end{array} \qquad \begin{array}{r} 7\ 0\ 0 \\ -\ 3\ 9\ 4 \\ \hline \end{array} \qquad \begin{array}{r} 4\ 0\ 0 \\ -\ 1\ 5\ 7 \\ \hline \end{array}$$

1.   Find the value.

1) 100 - 36 - 27 + 19 – 46 =   _____

2) 100 - 19 - 48 + 18 - 50 =   _____

3) 100 - 39 - 28 – 14 - 16 =   _____

4) 100 - 51 - 13 - 19 - 6 =   _____

5) 100 - 62 - 32 + 14 – 15 =   _____

6) 100 - 23 - 47 + 17 – 27 =   _____

2. What is the value of the 9 in each of these numbers? Circle the correct answer.

9247   a) Thousands   b) Hundreds   b) Tens   c) Ones

3968   a) Thousands   b) Hundreds   b) Tens   c) Ones

3. I read a ton of pages. It's a three-digit number. The hundreds digit is 1. The tens digit is four more than the hundreds digit. The ones digit is two more than the tens digit. How many pages did I read?

Answer: _____

1. <u>Subtract.</u>

875 - 325 = ___   650 - 225 = ___   425 - 175 = ___

575 - 125 = ___   850 - 625 = ___   325 - 75 = ___

2. <u>Find</u> the missing numbers.

? − 360 = 760   ? − 270 = 580

? = _____   ? = _____

3. <u>Add.</u>   Score: ___/8   Time: __ : __

$$\begin{array}{r} 2\ 7\ 5 \\ +\ 3\ 2\ 5 \\ \hline \end{array}$$
$$\begin{array}{r} 1\ 5\ 5 \\ +\ 2\ 4\ 5 \\ \hline \end{array}$$
$$\begin{array}{r} 4\ 2\ 5 \\ +\ 1\ 7\ 5 \\ \hline \end{array}$$
$$\begin{array}{r} 5\ 7\ 5 \\ +\ 1\ 2\ 5 \\ \hline \end{array}$$

$$\begin{array}{r} 4\ 5\ 5 \\ +\ 3\ 8\ 5 \\ \hline \end{array}$$
$$\begin{array}{r} 3\ 6\ 5 \\ +\ 4\ 5\ 5 \\ \hline \end{array}$$
$$\begin{array}{r} 5\ 5\ 5 \\ +\ 2\ 8\ 5 \\ \hline \end{array}$$
$$\begin{array}{r} 5\ 1\ 5 \\ +\ 2\ 9\ 5 \\ \hline \end{array}$$

4. <u>Fill in</u> the missing numbers. A number has to be more than

1.

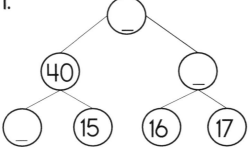
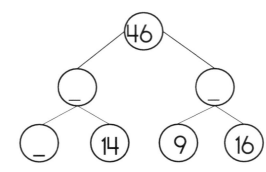

1. Subtract.

950 - 100 - 350 = _____   650 - 250 - 300 = _____

800 - 200 - 400 = _____   600 - 150 - 250 = _____

700 - 400 - 150 = _____   550 - 150 - 150 = _____

400 – 150 – 150 = _____   900 – 350 – 450 = _____

2. I'm building a solid slab of rocks: the two rocks next to each other are added to get the number up above. Fill in the missing numbers.

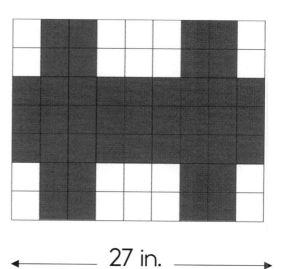

3. Count the squares below to find the perimeter of the whole square and the perimeter of the shaded shape.

27 in.

Answer: _____.

1. <u>Fill in</u> the missing numbers to make the equations true.

$$\underline{} + \underline{} + \underline{} = 36$$

$$\underline{} + \underline{} + \underline{} = 32$$

$$\underline{} + \underline{} + \underline{} = 27$$

2. <u>Add.</u>

```
  2 3 4        4 8 7        3 5  2        1 4 6
+ 3 6 7      + 1 3 7      + 3 6  9      + 4 3 9
```

3. <u>Subtract.</u>

```
  5 0 0        5 0 0        7 0 0        7 0 0
- 2 1 7      - 3 6 3      - 4 2 5      - 3 8 6
```

1. <u>Fill in</u> the missing "+", "-", or "=" to make the equations true. You can use the same sign ("+", "-", or "=") more than once.

12 _____ 14 _____ 15 _____ 17

56 _____ 18 _____ 7 _____ 31

85 _____ 46 _____ 35 _____ 96

95 _____ 73 _____ 17 _____ 39

2. <u>Continue</u> a series of numbers.

3, 5, 8, 12, _____, _____, _____, _____, _____, _____, _____.

96, 2, 94, 3, 92, 4, _____, _____, _____, _____.

120, 10, 110, 9, 101, 8, ____, _____, _____, _____, _____, ____.

1. <u>Add</u> or <u>subtract</u>.   Score ___/20   Time __:__

```
   1 1              1 1             1
   1 5 9           1 7 5           1 9 3           1 7 3
 + 2 6 4         + 3 8 6         + 3 4 2         + 3 5 7
 ---------       ---------       ---------       ---------
   4 2 3           5 6 1           5 3 5
```

```
   4 0 0           4 0 0           4 0 0           4 0 0
 - 1 7 1         - 2 4 8         - 1 3 5         - 2 6 9
 ---------       ---------       ---------       ---------
```

```
   2 4 6           2 7 9           2 5 8           2 3 5
 + 2 8 6         + 2 5 2         + 4 7 5         + 2 7 8
 ---------       ---------       ---------       ---------
```

```
   5 0 0           5 0 0           7 0 0           7 0 0
 - 1 4 8         - 2 3 9         - 1 5 7         - 2 6 3
 ---------       ---------       ---------       ---------
```

```
   3 6 4           3 7 7           3 1 5           3 8 6
 + 3 4 8         + 2 9 4         + 3 9 9         + 3 5 7
 ---------       ---------       ---------       ---------
```

1. <u>Add</u> or <u>subtract</u>.　　Score ___/20　　Time __:__

```
   4 1 3        5 2 7        3 2 8        3 0 4
 + 1 6 8      + 3 7 9      + 1 0 9      + 1 4 8
 _____     _____     _____     _____


   6 0 0        6 0 0        6 0 0        6 0 0
 - 3 4 1      - 1 9 8      - 4 2 5      - 3 5 9
 _____     _____     _____     _____


   4 7 1        5 2 6        4 7 1        3 8 4
 + 3 9 9      + 1 8 5      + 2 4 9      + 3 3 7
 _____     _____     _____     _____


   7 0 0        7 0 0        7 0 0        7 0 0
 - 3 6 9      - 3 9 4      - 6 1 5      - 4 9 6
 _____     _____     _____     _____


   5 1 6        6 3 1        5 4 8        6 8 3
 + 1 9 4      + 3 8 9      + 2 7 3      + 2 4 7
 _____     _____     _____     _____
```

1. <u>Add</u> or <u>subtract</u>.   Score ___/20   Time __:__

```
   6 4 1        5 9 7        4 7 9        6 3 6
 + 3 6 9      + 2 4 8      + 4 6 7      + 4 7 4
 _____      _____      _____      _____


   8 0 0        8 0 0        8 0 0        8 0 0
 - 4 7 5      - 7 4 2      - 5 8 5      - 5 1 2
 _____      _____      _____      _____


   4 1 7        8 3 5        2 6 4        9 4 6
 + 4 8 7      + 1 7 8      + 4 9 9      + 1 3 7
 _____      _____      _____      _____


   9 0 0        9 0 0        9 0 0        9 0 0
 - 3 8 7      - 5 1 3      - 6 4 5      - 7 2 6
 _____      _____      _____      _____


   2 7 4        1 0 7        4 8 2        9 0 4
 + 4 8 9      + 7 9 5      + 2 7 8      + 1 9 2
 _____      _____      _____      _____
```

1. Add or subtract.   Score ___/20   Time __:__

7 5 8	6 7 8	8 9 9	4 7 5
+ 2 4 4	+ 3 2 6	+ 3 5 2	+ 3 9 7

8 0 0	4 0 0	9 0 0	6 0 0
- 4 9 1	- 1 3 8	- 7 7 5	- 3 7 9

2 6 4	4 7 7	3 8 7	1 7 6
+ 8 6 9	+ 5 3 5	+ 7 6 9	+ 8 3 8

5 0 0	7 0 0	9 0 0	3 0 0
- 4 1 6	- 3 6 8	- 5 2 3	- 1 8 7

5 3 4	4 9 7	3 6 8	3 4 4
+ 3 9 6	+ 4 3 5	+ 8 6 9	+ 4 7 9

1. <u>Add</u> or <u>subtract</u>.　　Score ___/20　　Time __:__

```
    7 5 4        6 7 5        8 7 9        4 5 5
  + 5 9 4      + 5 6 6      + 1 5 6      + 7 9 6
  ─────────    ─────────    ─────────    ─────────


    9 0 0        5 0 0        9 0 0        7 0 0
  - 5 9 2      - 3 3 7      - 4 8 5      - 2 6 3
  ─────────    ─────────    ─────────    ─────────


    2 9 4        7 7 9        2 8 5        1 8 6
  + 5 6 7      + 5 4 5      + 7 7 9      + 4 3 4
  ─────────    ─────────    ─────────    ─────────


    6 0 0        8 0 0        6 0 0        8 0 0
  - 3 9 5      - 2 8 8      - 4 8 3      - 5 8 5
  ─────────    ─────────    ─────────    ─────────


    5 6 4        8 9 6        2 6 5        3 5 4
  + 4 9 7      + 4 5 5      + 8 8 9      + 7 7 2
  ─────────    ─────────    ─────────    ─────────
```

1. Add or subtract.   Score ___/20   Time __:__

```
   3 1 5        9 8 7        6 9 8        3 0 2
 + 6 4 9      + 3 1 4      + 5 3 8      + 9 7 7
 _____      _____      _____      _____


   7 9 6        5 7 3        7 2 0        3 0 4
 - 2 7 4      - 2 9 5      - 4 9 3      - 1 5 6
 _____      _____      _____      _____


   6 2 3        1 7 2        4 1 6        3 8 1
 + 2 8 7      + 8 9 8      + 8 0 4      + 1 4 9
 _____      _____      _____      _____


   8 0 3        7 0 6        5 0 7        7 0 9
 - 1 8 7      - 2 9 7      - 2 7 6      - 4 3 9
 _____      _____      _____      _____


   5 8 9        3 4 6        5 1 2        6 7 2
 + 9 7 6      + 8 7 3      + 9 7 9      + 7 9 7
 _____      _____      _____      _____
```

1. Add or subtract.   Score ___/20   Time __:__

$$\begin{array}{r} 6\;1\;4 \\ +\;6\;8\;9 \\ \hline \end{array} \qquad \begin{array}{r} 9\;9\;7 \\ +\;2\;1\;5 \\ \hline \end{array} \qquad \begin{array}{r} 6\;7\;8 \\ +\;7\;4\;6 \\ \hline \end{array} \qquad \begin{array}{r} 3\;8\;2 \\ +\;2\;5\;8 \\ \hline \end{array}$$

$$\begin{array}{r} 8\;9\;2 \\ -\;2\;3\;4 \\ \hline \end{array} \qquad \begin{array}{r} 8\;1\;2 \\ -\;2\;9\;5 \\ \hline \end{array} \qquad \begin{array}{r} 6\;2\;1 \\ -\;4\;3\;3 \\ \hline \end{array} \qquad \begin{array}{r} 8\;0\;1 \\ -\;1\;4\;6 \\ \hline \end{array}$$

$$\begin{array}{r} 5\;7\;3 \\ +\;1\;6\;8 \\ \hline \end{array} \qquad \begin{array}{r} 7\;2\;3 \\ +\;1\;9\;5 \\ \hline \end{array} \qquad \begin{array}{r} 3\;1\;5 \\ +\;4\;8\;5 \\ \hline \end{array} \qquad \begin{array}{r} 5\;4\;9 \\ +\;9\;3\;8 \\ \hline \end{array}$$

$$\begin{array}{r} 9\;0\;3 \\ -\;3\;8\;5 \\ \hline \end{array} \qquad \begin{array}{r} 7\;1\;6 \\ -\;4\;9\;8 \\ \hline \end{array} \qquad \begin{array}{r} 8\;0\;2 \\ -\;2\;4\;6 \\ \hline \end{array} \qquad \begin{array}{r} 7\;0\;4 \\ -\;3\;7\;9 \\ \hline \end{array}$$

$$\begin{array}{r} 4\;7\;6 \\ +\;2\;7\;8 \\ \hline \end{array} \qquad \begin{array}{r} 3\;9\;8 \\ +\;6\;9\;5 \\ \hline \end{array} \qquad \begin{array}{r} 4\;9\;7 \\ +\;5\;2\;4 \\ \hline \end{array} \qquad \begin{array}{r} 4\;8\;3 \\ +\;6\;0\;9 \\ \hline \end{array}$$

1. <u>Add</u> or <u>subtract</u>.   Score ___/20   Time __:__

```
   3 6 8          3 5 9          8 8 2          7 6 8
 + 1 4 5        + 1 9 3        + 8 7 4        + 3 4 5
 ────────       ────────       ────────       ────────


   7 2 5          3 0 8          7 8 3          9 7 6
 - 4 8 7        - 1 8 9        - 4 7 9        - 5 8 8
 ────────       ────────       ────────       ────────


   2 7 7          8 7 9          1 6 3          9 9 2
 + 7 1 8        + 1 4 4        + 3 6 8        + 7 5 4
 ────────       ────────       ────────       ────────


   5 0 7          9 0 1          6 0 3          8 0 5
 - 1 7 5        - 2 3 5        - 1 5 4        - 3 5 8
 ────────       ────────       ────────       ────────


   5 3 5          5 8 7          2 5 6          6 4 5
 + 2 6 9        + 3 3 6        + 4 6 7        + 3 3 5
 ────────       ────────       ────────       ────────
```

1. Add or subtract.   Score ___/20   Time __:__

3 7 8	8 9 3	8 4 2	4 6 7
+ 5 6 7	+ 6 7 3	+ 9 0 2	+ 5 6 8

9 3 6	5 3 5	8 4 6	9 8 7
- 5 8 9	- 1 6 7	- 3 5 7	- 4 9 8

6 8 5	9 6 7	4 8 3	6 9 6
+ 3 9 5	+ 7 8 4	+ 5 8 9	+ 2 6 4

8 3 1	9 0 5	7 8 5	7 9 1
- 3 9 3	- 4 8 5	- 2 9 9	- 4 8 7

3 1 4	6 2 5	4 8 3	6 8 9
+ 5 8 9	+ 6 7 8	+ 8 6 9	+ 9 4 6

1. <u>Subtract.</u>   Score ___/20   Time __:__

```
  10 0 0        10 0 0        10 0 0        10 0 0
-    2 2 5     -   1 5 6     -   7 3 4     -   5 1 9
```

```
  10 0 0        10 0 0        10 0 0        10 0 0
-    1 7 2     -   6 9 3     -   7 5 8     -   4 7 2
```

```
  10 0 0        10 0 0        10 0 0        10 0 0
-    5 8 5     -   4 5 9     -   5 3 1     -   7 1 6
```

```
  10 0 0        10 0 0        10 0 0        10 0 0
-    6 6 5     -   4 8 6     -   9 4 4     -   3 7 9
```

```
  10 0 0        10 0 0        10 0 0        10 0 0
-    6 7 4     -   4 3 1     -   2 8 9     -   7 4 5
```

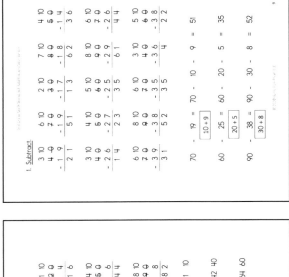

1. Circle the correct answer.

I have a series of numbers: 6, 7, 9, 12, ___ What is the next number?

a) 16   b) 17   c) 14

2. My brother and I played 30 games. If my brother played 10 games, how many games did I play?

Circle your answer.   a) 21   b) 40   c) 20

3. Write the missing numbers.

6000 + 200 + 40 + 5 = 6245
9000 + 500 + 30 + 1 = 9531
1000 + 0 + 20 + 5 = 1025
5000 + 300 + 70 + 8 = 5378
4000 + 200 + 0 + 4 = 4204
4000 + 100 + 30 + 7 = 4137
5000 + 500 + 50 + 7 = 5557
8000 + 700 + 30 + 4 = 8734

800 + 20 + 4 = 824
700 + 30 + 6 = 736
100 + 20 + 5 = 125
600 + 90 + 1 = 691
500 + 90 + 8 = 598
900 + 20 + 0 = 920
200 + 60 + 9 = 269
900 + 20 + 6 = 926

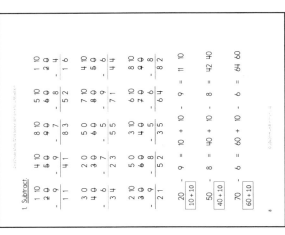

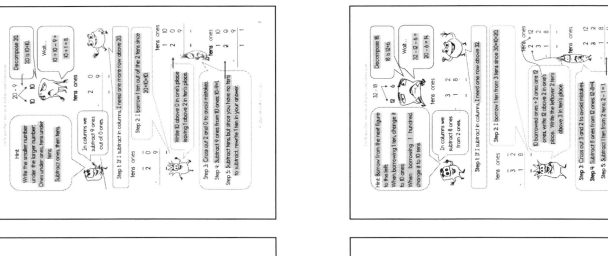

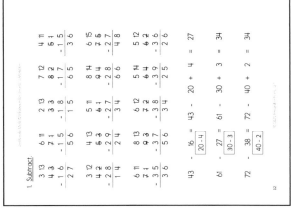

1. Solve the problems.

My sister has 13 pink ribbons, 8 blue ribbons, and 5 green ribbons. How many ribbons are there in all?

13 + 8 + 5 = 26 (ribbons in all)

In my class there are 26 kids. 9 kids like to read "Diary of a Wimpy Kid", and there 7 fewer kids who like to read "500 Awesome Facts" than who like to read "What Should Darla Do". How many kids like to read "500 Awesome Facts"?

26 - 9 = 17.   5 kids like to read "What Should Darla Do"

How many kids like to read "What Should Darla"

5 + 7 = 12 (kids who like to read "What Should Darla"

Using all digits 2, 5, 7 write all the six different numbers possible. Arrange the numbers up to the greatest number.

257, 275, 527, 572, 725, 752
257, 275, 527, 572, 725, 752

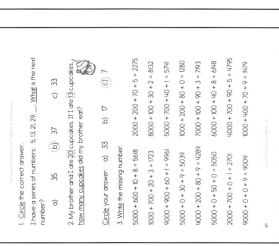

1. Circle the correct answer.

I have a series of numbers: 5, 13, 21, 29, ___ What is the next number?

a) 35   b) 37   c) 33

2. My brother and I ate 20 cupcakes. If I ate 13 cupcakes, how many cupcakes did my brother eat?

Circle your answer.   a) 33   b) 17   c) 7

3. Write the missing number.

5000 + 600 + 10 + 8 = 5618
1000 + 700 + 20 + 3 = 1723
9000 + 900 + 60 + 1 = 9961
5000 + 0 + 30 + 9 = 5039
4000 + 200 + 80 + 9 = 4289
6000 + 100 + 40 + 8 = 6148
2000 + 700 + 0 + 1 = 2701
9000 + 0 + 0 + 9 = 9009

2000 + 200 + 70 + 5 = 2275
8000 + 100 + 30 + 2 = 8132
5000 + 700 + 40 + 1 = 5741
1000 + 200 + 80 + 0 = 1280
7000 + 100 + 90 + 3 = 7193
4000 + 700 + 90 + 5 = 4795
4000 + 400 + 70 + 9 = 4479

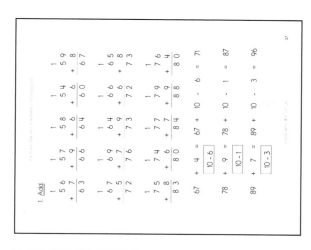

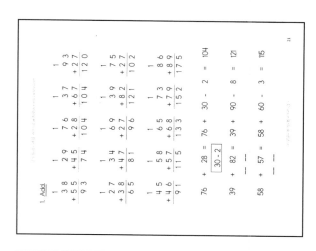

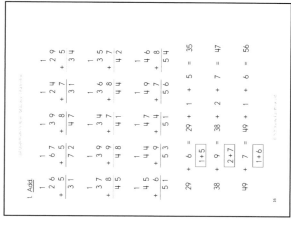

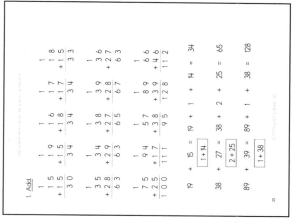

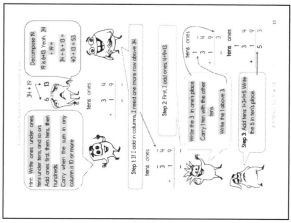

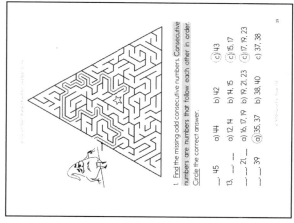

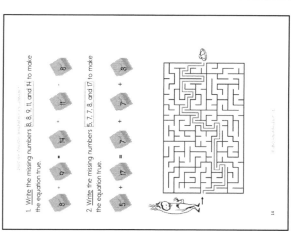

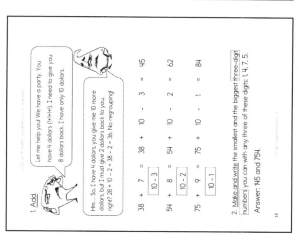

Panel 22

1. I added three addends to **5** and got **30**. Write the missing numbers to make the equations true.

5 + __ + __ + __ = 30

5 + __ + __ + __ = 30

> No trouble! I circle 5 bricks and arrange the leftover bricks in any order.

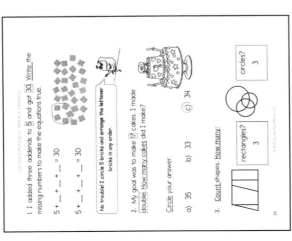

2. My goal was to make **17** cakes. I made double. How many cakes did I make?
Circle your answer.
a) 35   b) 33   c) 34

3. Count shapes. How many?

rectangles? 3

circles? 3

Panel 23

1. Find the missing numbers.

Remember: Whole = Part + Part2

😊 -3 = 47   😊 -2 = 78
😊 = 50   😊 -8 = 52

? -4 = 26   ? -6 = 44   😊 -9 = 81
? = 30   ? = 50   ? = 90

🐻 -5 = 65   😊 -7 = 23   😊 -1 = 39
? = 70   ? -2 = 70   😊 -4 = 40

2. How many of each shape? Color the boxes for each number on the graph.

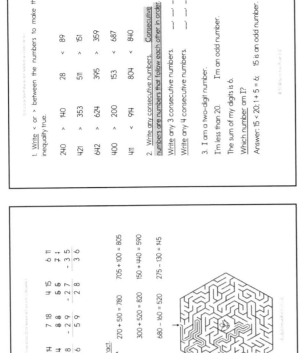

Panel 24

1. Subtract.

```
 3 15     2 14     7 18     4 15     6 11
 4 5      3 4      8 8      5 5      7 1
-1 7     -1 8     -2 9     -2 7     -3 5
 2 8      1 6      5 9      2 8      3 6
```

2. Add or subtract.

400 + 200 = 600   270 + 510 = 780   705 + 100 = 805
637 + 300 = 937   300 + 520 = 820   150 + 440 = 590
490 - 220 = 270   680 - 160 = 520   275 - 130 = 145

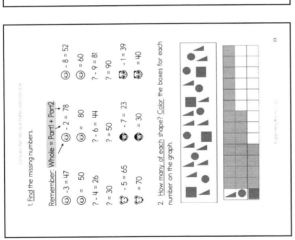

Panel 25

1. Write < or > between the numbers to make the inequality true.

240 > 140   28 < 89
421 > 353   511 > 151
642 > 624   395 > 359
400 > 200   153 < 687
411 < 914   804 < 840

2. Write any consecutive numbers. Consecutive numbers are numbers that follow each other in order.

Write any 3 consecutive numbers. ___ ___ ___

Write any 4 consecutive numbers. ___ ___ ___ ___

3. I am a two-digit number.
I'm less than 20.
The sum of my digits is 6.
Which number am I?
Answer: 15 < 20; 1 + 5 = 6;   15 is an odd number.

Panel 26

1. I added two addends to **8** and got **30**. Write the missing numbers to make the equations true.

8 + __ + __ = 30

8 + __ + __ = 30

2. I met **7** squirrels on Friday. On Saturday, the number of squirrels I met increased by **8**. The number of squirrels I met on Sunday was **8** more than that of Friday. How many squirrels did I meet in all?
Circle your answer.
a) 35   b) 33   c) 34

7+8=15 (Sat) 7+8=15 (Sun) 7+8+15=35 (squirrels)

3. Continue the pattern.

99, 88, 77, 66, 55, 44, 33, 22, 11

4. Write the number from the choice box to make the inequality true.

253 < ___ < 279

a) 251   b) 289   c) 265

Panel 27

1. Write the missing numbers **8, 9, 12, 13, and 26** to make the equation true.

26 + 8 = 12 + 13 + ...

2. Find the route. You can go only right or down at each turn.

Start →	+6	+4	-8	+5
-4	+9	-5	+6	+3
-2	+7	+5	-9	+6
-2	-8	+1	+1	-4
+7	+8	+2	-3	Finish = 15

3. Write the missing numbers **9, 10, 12, 13, and 18** to make the equation true.

Panel 28

1. Subtract.   Score: ___/15   Time: ___:___

```
 1 14     2 13     7 11     4 12     6 15
 2 4      3 3      8 1      5 2      7 5
-1 6     -1 5     -4 8     -3 7     -2 8
   8      1 8      3 3      1 5      4 7

 3 12     4 13     5 11     8 14     5 12
 4 2      5 3      6 4      9 4      6 2
-2 8     -2 9     -2 7     -2 8     -2 7
 1 4      2 4      3 4      6 6      4 8

 6 11     8 13     6 12     5 14     5 12
 7 1      9 3      7 2      6 4      6 2
-3 5     -3 7     -3 8     -3 9     -3 6
 3 6      3 4      3 4      2 5      2 6
```

43 - 16 =   43 - 20 + 4 = 27

61 - 27 =   61 - 30 + 3 = 34

72 - 38 =   72 - 40 + 2 = 34

Panel 29

1. Circle the correct answer.
I have a series of numbers: 2, 7, 9, 14, 16, 21, 19, 24, ___
What is the next number?
a) 20   b) 22   c) 29

2. I have some numbers and signs: 15, 5, 10, +, -.
Write the equation that equals one of the answer choices. Circle the correct answer.
_____
a) 0   b) 30   c) 5

I have some numbers and signs: 27, 5, 12, +, -.
Write the equation that equals one of the answer choices. Circle the correct answer.
_____
a) 44   b) 31   c) 34

3. Circle an even number to make the statements true.

18 < ___ < 34   a) 12   b) 8   c) 25   d) 32

64 < ___ < 80   a) 78   b) 102   c) 48   d) 56

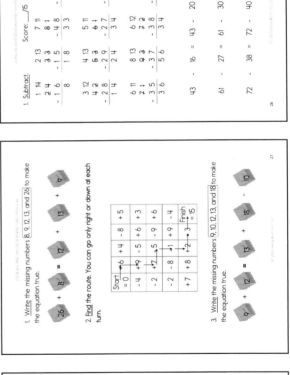

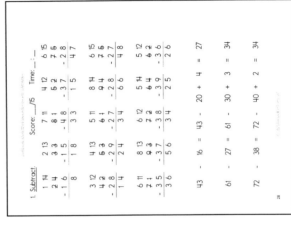

Left column — page 33

1. Find the missing numbers.

? - 200 = 300   ? - 100 = 700
? - 300 = 600   ? = 800
? = 500   ? = 900

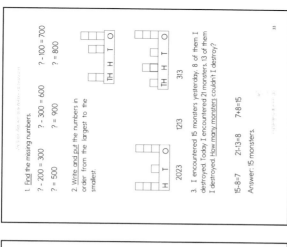

	TH	H	T	O
2023				
1213				
313				

2. Write and put the numbers in order from the largest to the smallest.

3. I encountered 15 monsters yesterday. 8 of them I destroyed. Today I encountered 21 monsters. 13 of them I destroyed. How many monsters couldn't I destroy?

15-8=7   21-13=8   7+8=15

Answer: 15 monsters.

Left column — page 32

1. Subtract:

```
 4 11    6 13    3 10    7 12    5 17
 5 1     7 3     4 0     8 2     6 7
-2 4    -4 7    -1 5    -5 9    -3 9
 2 7     2 6     2 5     2 3     2 8
```

2. I have some numbers and signs:
14, 7, 21, +, -.

Write the equation that equals one of the answer choices. Circle the correct answer.

a) 29   b) 24   (c) 14

3. What is the value of the 5 in each of these numbers? Circle the correct answer.

3591 a) Thousands (b) Hundreds b) Tens c) Ones
2658 a) Thousands b) Hundreds (b) Tens c) Ones
5902 (a) Thousands b) Hundreds b) Tens c) Ones
3665 a) Thousands b) Hundreds b) Tens (c) Ones

Left column — page 31

1. Add:

```
  1       1       8       1      7 5
 2 5     6 4     8 3     3 7    +1 8
+3 9    +2 8    +1 7    +5 4     9 3
 6 4     9 2   1 0 0     9 1
```

2.

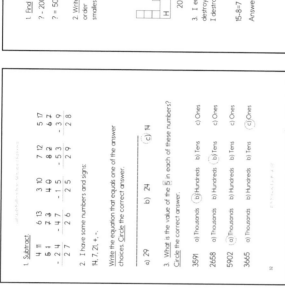

I wanted to use 18 blocks to build a tower but I used double. How many blocks did I use?

Answer: 18 + 18 = 36 (blocks)

3. Find the missing even consecutive numbers. Consecutive numbers are numbers that follow each other in order. Circle the correct answer.

__, __, 28   a) 28   b) 26   c) 24
16, __, __   a) 12, 14   b) 18, 20   c) 17, 18
__, __, 32, __   a) 30, 31, 34   b) 28, 30, 33   c) 28, 30, 34
__, __, 50   a) 30, 31, 34   b) 46, 48   b) 48, 49   c) 40, 44

Left column — page 30

1. Subtract:

```
 6 11    4 13    5 10    3 12    8 17
 7 1     5 3     6 0     4 2     9 7
-4 9    -3 5    -1 7    -2 4    -5 8
 2 2     4 3     4 3     1 8     3 9
```

2. I added two addends to 6 and got 31. Write the missing numbers to make the equations true.

6 + __ + __ = 31
6 + __ + __ = 31

3. I read 9 pages on Friday. On Saturday I read 12 pages. The number of pages I read on Sunday was 7 less than that of Friday and Saturday. How many pages did I read in all? Circle the correct answer.

9 + 12 + (9 + 12 - 7) = 35

a) 31   b) 34   (c) 35

4. Find the missing numbers.

? + 200 = 700   ? + 400 = 900   ? + 100 = 700
? = 500   ? = 500   ? = 600

Right column — page 37

1. Subtract: Score: __/15   Time: __:__

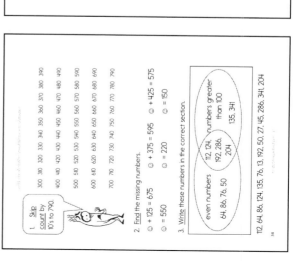

Right column — page 36

1. Continue the pattern:

98, 94, 88, 80, 70, 58, 44, 28, 10.

2. Circle the right answer.

A: 41 - 25 + 19   a) A is greater than B
B: 41 + 19 - 25   b) A is less than B
                   (c) A is equal to B

A: 91 - 67   a) A is greater than B
B: 78 - 39   (b) A is less than B
                   c) A is equal to B

3. Find out what number is hiding.

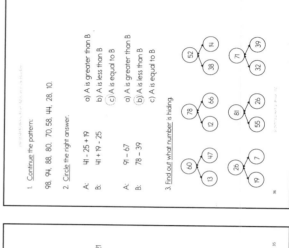

52 → 38, 14
71 → 32, 39
78 → 66, 12
81 → 26, 55
60 → 47, 13
26 → 7, 19

Right column — page 35

1. Add:

```
  1       1       1      7 7
 6 6     8 8     3 3    +1 6
+1 5    +2 7    +1 9     9 3
 8 1    1 1 5    5 2
```

2. Find the missing numbers.

? - 125 = 673   ? - 314 = 254   ? - 423 = 521
? = 798   ? = 568   ? = 944

3. Circle the right answer.

A: 45 - 29   a) A is greater than B
B: 23 + 19   (b) A is less than B
                   c) A is equal to B

A: 25 + 47 - 36   a) A is greater than B
B: 70 - 48 + 14   b) A is less than B
                   (c) A is equal to B

A: 54 - 19   (a) A is greater than B
B: 82 - 65   b) A is less than B
                   c) A is equal to B

Right column — page 34

1. Skip count by 10's to 790.

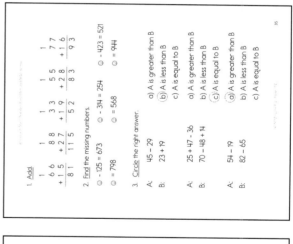

300 310 320 330 340 350 360 370 380 390
400 410 420 430 440 450 460 470 480 490
500 510 520 530 540 550 560 570 580 590
600 610 620 630 640 650 660 670 680 690
700 710 720 730 740 750 760 770 780 790

2. Find the missing numbers.

? + 125 = 675   ? + 375 = 595   ? + 425 = 575
? = 550   ? = 220   ? = 150

3. Write these numbers in the correct section.

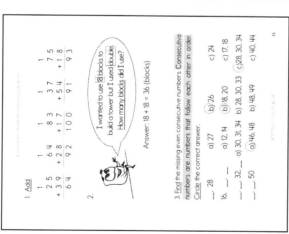

even numbers: 64, 86, 76, 50
204
numbers greater than 100: 112, 124, 192, 286, 135, 341

112, 64, 86, 124, 135, 76, 13, 192, 50, 27, 45, 286, 341, 204

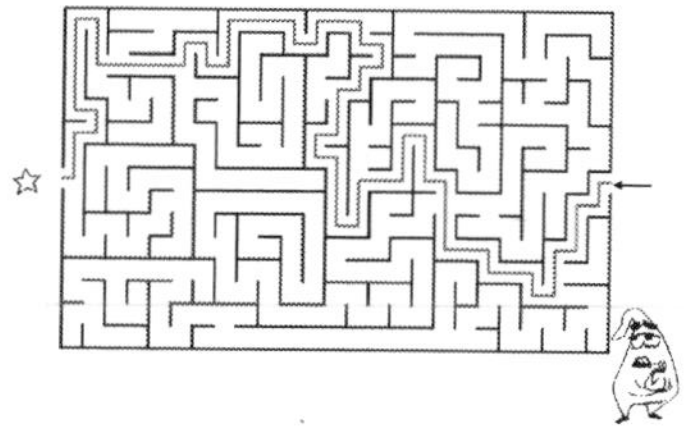

(Page 41)

1. Subtract: Score: ___ /12 Time: __:__

```
 6 9 10      2 9 10      4 9 10      3 9 10
 7 0 0       3 0 0       5 0 0       4 0 0
-1 6 7      -1 8 6      -2 7 1      -2 8 9
-----       -----       -----       -----
 5 3 3       1 1 4       2 2 9       1 1 1

 5 9 10      7 9 10      2 9 10
 6 0 0       8 0 0       3 0 0
-3 2 7      -5 4 5      -1 2 4
-----       -----       -----
 2 7 3       3 5 5       1 7 6

 3 9 10      5 9 10      6 9 10
 4 0 0       6 0 0       7 0 0
-1 5 8      -5 1 7      -3 9 9
-----       -----       -----
 2 4 2       1 7 9       3 0 1
```

2. My brother and I have 65 dollars altogether. If I have 29 dollars more, how many dollars does he have? Circle the correct answer.

65-29=36   18+18=36

a) 21   b) 19   c) 18 *(c circled)*

(Page 40)

1. Subtract: Score: ___ /12 Time: __:__

```
 8 9 10      7 9 10      5 9 10
 9 0 0       8 0 0       6 0 0
-3 2 5      -2 2 5      -3 8 1
-----       -----       -----
 5 7 5       5 7 5       2 1 9

 4 9 10      8 9 10      2 9 10
 5 0 0       9 0 0       3 0 0
-2 8 4      -7 3 8      -1 9 2
-----       -----       -----
 2 1 6       1 6 2       1 0 8

 6 9 10      3 9 10
 7 0 0       4 0 0
-4 7 2      -1 6 8
-----       -----
 2 2 8       2 3 2
```

2. I used 41 rocks yesterday, 13 of them hit the target. Today I used 34 rocks. 19 of them hit the target. How many more or less rocks hit the target yesterday?

41 - 13 = 28 (yesterday)   34 - 19 = 15 (today)

28 - 15 = 13

Answer: 13 rocks more.

(Page 39)

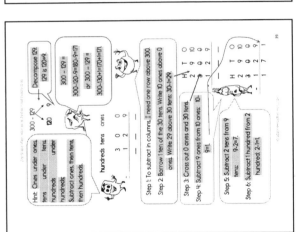

300 - 129

Decompose 129. 129 is 120+9

300 - 129 = 300-120-9=171 or 300 - 129 = 171

300-130+1=170+1=171

Hint: Ones under ones, tens under tens, hundreds under hundreds. Subtract ones, then tens, then hundreds.

Step 1: To subtract in columns, I need one row above 300.

Step 2: Borrow 1 ten of the 30 tens. Write 10 ones above 0 ones. Write 29 above 30 tens: 30=10+29

Step 3: Cross out 0 ones and 30 tens.

Step 4: Subtract 9 ones from 10 ones: 10-9=1

Step 5: Subtract 2 tens from 9 tens: 9-2=7

Step 6: Subtract 1 hundred from 2 hundred: 2-1=1

(Page 38)

1. I'm building a solid wall of rocks: the two rocks next to each other are added to get the number up above. Fill in the missing numbers.

```
            [106]
        [51]    [55]
     [24]  [27]  [28]
   [11] [13] [14] [14]
  [7]  [4]  [9]  [5]  [9]
```

2. Subtract.

600 - 300 = 300   900-600=300   800-500=300
700 - 600 = 100   700-300=400   400-300=100
900 - 400 = 500   800-200=600   300-200=100
800 - 400 = 400   600-400=200   900-100=800
600 - 200 = 400   400-100=300   800-300=500

3. Compare and find out how many more or less the numbers are different by.

100 > 50 by 50   30 < 60 by 30
70 > 10 by 60   40 < 90 by 50
60 > 20 by 40   50 < 70 by 20

(Page 45)

1. Round each number to the nearest 10. Look at the next digit to the right. If it is 0, 1, 2, 3, or 4 then ROUND DOWN. If it is 5, 6, 7, 8, 9 then, ROUND UP. The first one is done for you.

243 240   471 470   216 220   591 590
827 830   379 380   740 740   655 660

2. Round each number to the nearest 100. Look at the next digit to the right. If it is 0, 1, 2, 3, or 4 then, ROUND DOWN. If it is 5, 6, 7, 8, 9 then ROUND UP. The first one is done for you.

235 200   449 400   167 200   518 500
873 900   395 400   720 700   657 700

3. Circle the right answer.

__8 + 4 = 82   a) 5   b) 3   c) 6

53 + 3 = 91   a) 7   b) 9   c) 8 *(c circled)*

38 + 27 = __5   a) 8   b) 5   c) 6 *(c circled)*

(Page 44)

1. Subtract.

800 - 250 = 550   1000 - 350 = 650
900 - 450 = 450   1000 - 750 = 250
700 - 550 = 150   500 - 150 = 350
600 - 350 = 250   1000 - 550 = 450
400 - 150 = 250   800 - 450 = 350
900 - 650 = 250   700 - 350 = 350

2. Fill in the missing numbers to make the equations true.

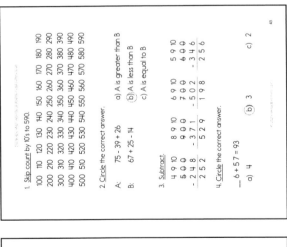

15 + 15 + 15 = 45

15 + 15 + 9 = 39

15 + 9 + 8 = 32

(Page 43)

1. Skip count by 10s to 590.

100 110 120 130 140 150 160 170 180 190
200 210 220 230 240 250 260 270 280 290
300 310 320 330 340 350 360 370 380 390
400 410 420 430 440 450 460 470 480 490
500 510 520 530 540 550 560 570 580 590

2. Circle the correct answer.

A: 75 - 39 + 26   a) A is greater than B
B: 67 + 25 - 14   b) A is less than B *(circled)*
                   c) A is equal to B

3. Subtract.

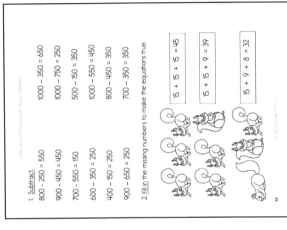

```
 4 9 10      8 9 10      6 9 10      5 9 10
 5 0 0       9 0 0       7 0 0       6 0 0
-2 4 8      -3 7 1      -5 0 2      -3 4 6
-----       -----       -----       -----
 2 5 2       5 2 9       1 9 8       2 5 6
```

4. Circle the correct answer.

__6 + 57 = 93   a) 4   b) 3   c) 2 *(b circled)*

(Page 42)

1. Arrange the numbers from the least to the greatest. The first one is done for you.

34	87	25	96	54	13	76	102	94	37	65	41	59
13	25	34	37	41	54	59	65	76	87	94	96	102

2. Add or subtract.

712 + 26 = 738   521 + 73 = 594   918 + 31 = 949
624 + 25 = 649   346 + 52 = 398   253 + 36 = 289
433 - 33 = 400   862 - 41 = 821   528 - 25 = 503
848 - 36 = 812   268 - 51 = 217   729 - 27 = 702

3. Subtract. Hint: 710 - 160 = 710 - 200 + 40 = __

710 - 160 = 550   820 - 470 = 350   320 - 170 = 150
540 - 490 = 50   640 - 390 = 250   960 - 280 = 680
650 - 380 = 270   430 - 160 = 270   830 - 790 = 40

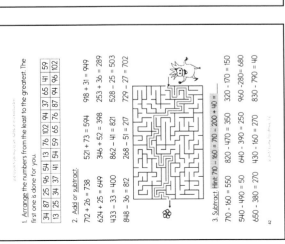

Page 50

1. Fill in the missing numbers. 1 letter is 1 digit (tens or ones).

A6 + 38 = 75   4C + D2 = 91   15E + 4F = G00
3 6 + 3 9 = 75   4 9 + 4 2 = 91   15 4 + 1 4 6 = _ 00

A6 + 4B = 120   3C + D9 = 86   6E + F9 = G00
7 6 + 4 4 = 120   3 7 + 4 9 = 86   6 1 + 3 9 = _ 00

2. Answer the questions.

Find the missing 1 even consecutive number. 26, 28.

Find the missing 2 odd consecutive numbers. 15, 17, 19

Find the missing 2 even consecutive numbers. 28, 30, 32

3. Subtract. Hint: 325 - 175 = 325 - 125 - 50 = 200 - 50 = 150.

950 - 250 = 700   750 - 30 = 720   400 - 350 = 50
675 - 225 = 450   950 - 425 = 525   625 - 375 = 250

Page 49

Score: ___/12 Time: ___:___

1. Subtract:

```
 6 10 14     2 11 18     4 12 13     3 11 15
   7  1  4     3  2  8     5  3  3     4  2  5
 - 1  9  6   - 1  3  9   - 2  7  5   - 2  3  6
 --------    --------    --------    --------
   5  1  8     1  8  9     2  5  8     1  8  9

 5 10 15     7 11 12     8 13 11     2 15 13
   6  1  5     8  2  2     9  4  1     3  6  3
 - 3  4  6   - 4  6  4   - 5  7  2   - 1  9  5
 --------    --------    --------    --------
   2  6  9     3  5  8     3  6  9     1  6  8

 3 13 12     4 16 14     5 18 11     6 16 17
   4  4  2     5  7  4     6  9  1     7  7  7
 - 1  6  3   - 3  8  7   - 5  9  2   - 4  8  8
 --------    --------    --------    --------
   2  7  9     1  8  7        9  9     2  8  9
```

2. Choose any of the three digits to make the total as close as possible to 500. Circle the correct answer.

197 + _____ = 500

a) 1, 9, 8   b) 2, 5, 6   c) 0, 3, 3

Page 48

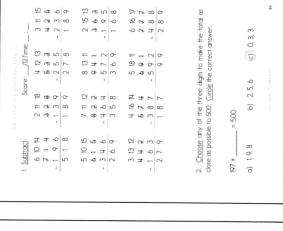
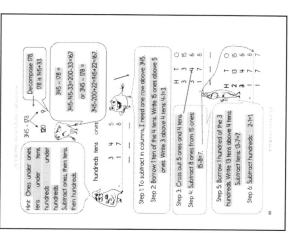
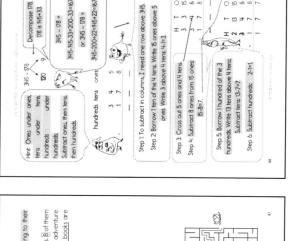

Decompose 178.
178 is 145+33

345 - 178

345 - 178 =
345-145-33=200-33=167
or 345 - 178 =
345-200+22=145+22=167

Hint: Ones under ones, tens under tens, hundreds under hundreds. Subtract ones, then tens, then hundreds.

Step 1: To subtract in columns, I need one row above 345.
Step 2: Borrow 1 ten of the 4 tens. Write 15 ones above 5 ones. Write 3 above 4 tens. 4=1+3.
Step 3: Cross out 5 ones and 4 tens.
Step 4: Subtract 8 ones from 15 ones. 15-8=7.
Step 5: Borrow 1 hundred of the 3 hundreds. Write 13 tens above 4 tens. Subtract tens: 13-7=7.
Step 6: Subtract hundreds. 2-1=1.

Page 47

1. Venn Diagram helps you sort things according to their different features.

I have many books. 10 of them are fantasy blocks. 8 of them are adventure books. 6 of them are fantasy and adventure books. 7 of them are history books. How many books are there? Fill in the diagram.

fantasy 10-6=4   both 6   adventure 8-6-2

history 7

Answer: 4 + 6 + 2 + 7 = 19 (books).

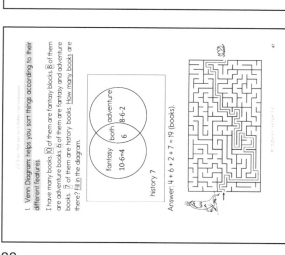

Page 54

1. Use < or > to make these statements true.

46 < 75 > 26   246 > 169 < 762
13 < 96 < 132   35 > 12 < 86
75 > 21 < 59   70 > 24 < 65
164 < 200 > 97   416 > 235 < 102

2. Write these numbers in order, from the smallest to the largest.

637, 120, 371, 97, 481, 56, 972, 40
40, 56, 97, 120, 371, 481, 637, 972

111, 842, 37, 890, 75, 614, 89, 201
37, 75, 89, 111, 201, 614, 842, 890

3. Add

```
  227      409      840      712
+ 131    + 350    + 125    + 226
-----    -----    -----    -----
  358      759      965      938
```

Page 53

1. Tallying, tally marks help you keep track of numbers in groups of five.

I have two brothers and two sisters. This graph shows the number of dollars collected by each of us.

	Dollars
Jack	IIII
Oliver	IIII IIII
James	IIII IIII
Emma	IIII IIII IIII
Evelyn	IIII IIII

How many dollars do the boys have?
39 dollars

How many dollars do Oliver and James have altogether?
24 dollars

How many more dollars does Emma have than Evelyn?
6 more dollars

What is the total number of dollars?
15+15+9+14+8=61 (dollars)

2. Continue a series of numbers.

2, 8, 5, 11, 8, 14, 11, 17, 14, 20, 17.
4, 9, 15, 22, 30, 39, 49, 60, 72, 85, 99.

Page 52

1. Find the missing numbers.

100 - ⊙ = 7   100 - ⊙ = 2
⊙ = 93   ⊙ = 98
100 - ⊙ = 8   100 - ? = 1
⊙ = 92   ? = 99
100 - ? = 6   ? = 96
? = 94
100 - ⊙ = 5   100 - ⊙ = 9
⊙ = 95   ⊙ = 91
? = 97

2. Fill in the missing numbers to make the equations true.

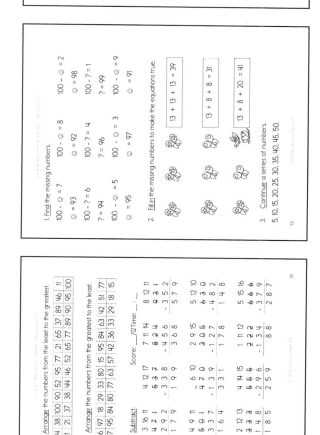

13 + 13 + 13 = 39

13 + 8 + 8 = 31

13 + 8 + 20 = 41

3. Continue a series of numbers.

5, 10, 15, 20, 25, 30, 35, 40, 45, 50.

Page 51

Score: ___ Time: ___:___

1. Arrange the numbers from the least to the greatest.

44 38 100 90 52 95 77 21 65 37 89 46 11
11 21 37 38 44 46 52 65 77 89 90 95 100

2. Arrange the numbers from the greatest to the least.

36 97 18 29 33 80 15 95 84 63 42 51 77
97 95 84 80 77 63 57 42 36 33 29 18 15

3. Subtract:

```
 4 12 17     7  1 14     8 12 11
   5  3  2     8  2  4     9  3  1
 - 3  3  8   - 4  5  6   - 3  5  2
 --------    --------    --------
   1  9  9     3  6  8     5  7  9

 4  9 11     2  9 15     5 12 10     5 15 16
   5  0  1     3  0  5     6  3  0     6  6  4
 - 4  7  0   - 1  2  7   - 4  8  2   - 1  3  4
 --------    --------    --------    --------
   1  6  4     1  7  8     1  4  8     5  3  0

 2 12 13     4  4 15     1 11 12
   3  3  3     5  6  6     2  2  2
 - 1  4  8   - 2  9  6   - 1  3  4
 --------    --------    --------
   1  8  5     2  5  9        8  8
```

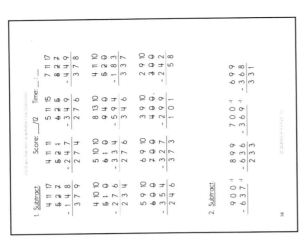
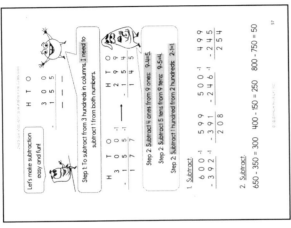
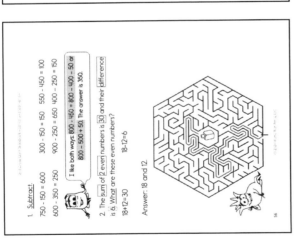
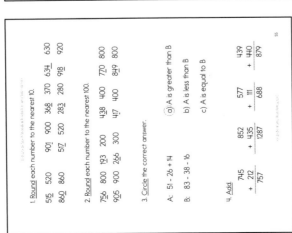
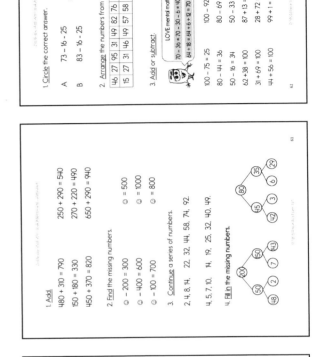
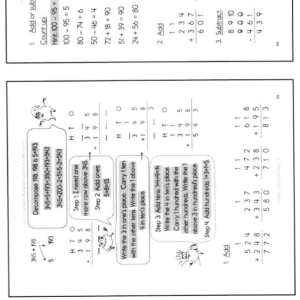

Page 63

1. Subtract. The first one is done for you.

Strategy: 164 - 70 = 164 - 100 + 30 = 64 + 30 = 94 ☺

141 - 50 = 41 + 50 = 91
137 - 80 = 37 + 20 = 57
129 - 40 = 29 + 60 = 89
105 - 96 = 5 + 4 = 9
104 - 96 = 4 + 4 = 8
101 - 92 = 1 + 8 = 9

150 - 65 = 50 + 35 = 85   161 - 92 = 61 + 8 = 69
154 - 99 = 54 + 1 = 55   172 - 93 = 72 + 7 = 79
185 - 98 = 85 + 2 = 87   153 - 97 = 53 + 3 = 56

2. Count the squares below to find the perimeter of the whole square and the perimeter of the shaded shape.

Perimeter is the distance around the shape. Hint: To find the perimeter of a rectangle, you need to add the lengths of the rectangle's four sides.

Perimeter s = 14+14+14+14=56 (in)

Answer:

P shape = 8+8+20+20=56 (in).

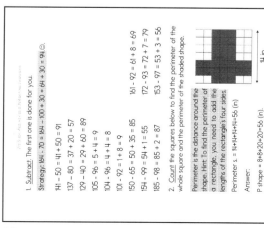

14 in.

Page 64

1. Add   Score: ___/8   Time: ___:___

```
 1 1         1 1         1 1
 9 2 5       6 9 3       7 9 6
+3 8 6      +1 4 7      +2 4 6
-------     -------     -------
1 3 1 1      8 4 0      1 0 4 2

 1 1         1 1         1 1
 6 4 5       5 3 5       6 7 5
+2 7 5      +1 9 8      +4 3 6
-------     -------     -------
 9 2 0       7 3 3      1 1 1 1
```

2. Choose any of the three digits to make the total as close as possible to 650. Circle the correct answer.

345 + 305 = 650

a) 3, 5, 5   b) 2, 0, 5   c) 3, 5, 0

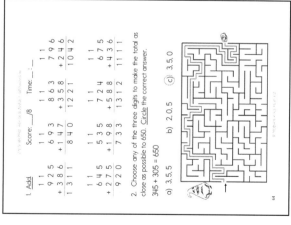

Page 65

1. I have several shapes. The perimeter of each is 41 feet. In each picture one of the measurements has disappeared. Write the length that should be on the missing side.

5 ft. 9 ft. P = 41 13 ft. 6 ft. ? ft. 8
9 ft. 4 ft. P = 41 8 ft. 5 ft. 6 ft. 5 ft. ? ft. 4

2. Last time I used a ton of blocks. You can write the number written as the largest possible number that you can make by using the digits 0, 1, 3. How many blocks did I use?

Answer: 30 blocks.

3. Fill in the missing "+", "-", or "=" to make the equations true. You can use the sign ("+", "-", or "=") more than once.

6 = 8 + 10 - 12   5 + 9 - 7 = 7
11 - 5 + 4 = 10   15 - 6 + 3 = 12
16 = 7 + 19 - 10   22 + 9 - 7 = 24

Page 66

1. Find the missing consecutive numbers. Circle the correct answer.

20. ___   A) 21.22   B) 23.25   C) 22.24
___ 44.   A) 38.36   B) 38.40   C) 40.42
___ 68.___   A) 70.72   B) 66.70   C) 66.72

2. Add

120 + 330 = 450   350 + 490 = 840   450 + 170 = 620
160 + 630 = 790   750 + 160 = 910   350 + 260 = 610
540 + 240 = 780   850 + 80 = 930   350 + 380 = 730

3. Find the missing numbers.

? - 125 = 672   ? - 375 = 225   ? - 425 = 575
? = 797   ? = 600   ? = 1000

4. Write the number.

Which value is equal to 20 tens?   200
Which value is equal to 52 hundreds?   5200

Page 67

1. Find the missing addend.

Hint: 40 - 13 = 40 - 10 - 3 = 40 - 13 = 40 - 20 + 7 = 27

① + 13 = 40   ⑤ + 42 = 80   ⑨ + 28 = 70
? = 27   ? = 38   ? = 42
② + 84 = 100   ⑥ + 56 = 70   ⑩ + 39 = 50
? = 16   ? = 14   ? = 11
③ + 75 = 90   ⑦ + 97 = 100   ⑪ + 61 = 80
? = 15   ? = 3   ? = 19

2. I spent 91 arrows to destroy the spiders. My brother used 23 arrows less than I used. If my sister used 48 arrows less than I used, how many arrows did we use altogether? Circle the correct answer.

a) 200   b) 196   c) 202

3. Subtract.

```
 7 9 10      6 9 10      3 9 10
 8 0 0       7 0 0       4 0 0
-6 2 9      -3 9 4      -1 5 7
-------     -------     -------
 1 7 1       3 0 6       2 4 3
```

Page 68

1. Find the value.

1) 100 - 36 - 27 + 19 - 46 = 10
2) 100 - 19 - 48 + 18 - 50 = 1
3) 100 - 39 - 28 - 14 - 16 = 3
4) 100 - 51 - 13 - 19 - 6 = 11
5) 100 - 62 - 32 + 14 - 15 = 5
6) 100 - 23 - 47 + 17 - 27 = 20

2. What is the value of the 9 in each of these numbers? Circle the correct answer.

9247   a) Thousands   b) Hundreds   c) Tens   c) Ones
3968   a) Thousands   b) Hundreds   b) Tens   c) Ones

3. I read a ton of pages. It's a three-digit number. The hundreds digit is 1. The tens digit is four more than the hundreds digit. The ones digit is two more than the tens digit. How many pages did I read?

Answer: 157 books.

Page 69

1. Subtract.

875 - 325 = 550   650 - 225 = 425   425 - 175 = 250
575 - 125 = 450   575 - 625 = 225   325 - 75 = 250

2. Find the missing numbers.

? - 360 = 760   ? - 270 = 580
? = 980   ? = 850

3. Add   Score: ___/8   Time: ___:___

```
 1 1         1 1         1 1
 2 7 5       4 2 5       5 7 5
+3 2 5      +1 7 5      +1 2 5
-------     -------     -------
 6 0 0       6 0 0       7 0 0

 1 1         1 1         1 1
 4 5 5       3 6 5       5 1 5
+3 8 5      +2 8 5      +2 9 5
-------     -------     -------
 8 4 0       8 4 0       8 1 0
```

4. Fill in the missing numbers. A number has to be more than 1.

46 → 25, 16 → 9, 14; 21, 7
73 → 33, 17 → 15, 40; 25

Page 70

1. Subtract.

950 - 100 - 350 = 500   650 - 250 - 300 = 100
800 - 200 - 400 = 200   600 - 150 - 250 = 200
700 - 400 - 150 = 150   550 - 150 - 150 = 250
400 - 150 - 150 = 100   900 - 350 - 450 = 100

2. I am building a solid slab of rocks: the two rocks next to each other are added to get the number up above. Fill in the missing numbers.

167
81   86
41   40   46
21   20   20   26
9   12   8   12   14

3. Count the squares below to find the perimeter of the whole square and the perimeter of the shaded shape.

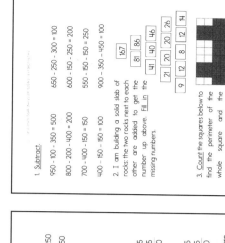

27 in.

P = 27+27+21+21=96 (in)

Answer: P=9+9+9+51=120 (in).

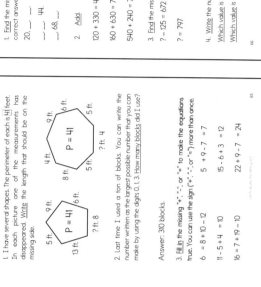
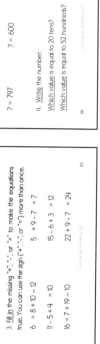

Page 71

1. Fill in the missing numbers to make the equations true.

$12 + 12 + 12 = 36$

$12 + 12 + 8 = 32$

$12 + 8 + 7 = 27$

2. Add.

```
  2 3 4        4 8 7        6 9 10
+ 3 6 7      + 1 3 7      + 3 5 2
  6 0 1        6 2 4        7 2 1
```

```
  4 9 10       6 9 10
+ 3 6 9      + 4 3 9
  5 8 5        8 6 5
```

3. Subtract.

```
  5 0 0        6 9 10
- 2 1 7      - 3 6 3
  2 8 3        3 1 4
```

Page 72

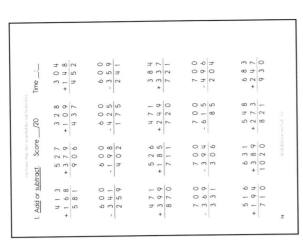

1. Fill in the missing "+", "–", or "=" to make the equations true.
You can use the same sign ("+", "–", or "=") more than once.

$12 = 14 + 15 - 17$

$56 - 18 - 7 = 31$

$85 + 46 - 35 = 96$

$95 = 73 - 17 + 39$

2. Continue a series of numbers.

3, 5, 8, 12, 17, 23, 30, 38, 47, 57, __68__.

96, 2, __94__, 3, __92__, 4, __90__, 5, __88__, 6.

__120__, 10, __110__, 9, __101__, 8, __93__, 7, __86__, 6, __80__, 5, __75__

Page 73

1. Add or subtract. Score ___/20   Time __:__

```
  1 5 9      1 7 5      1 9 3      1 7 3
+ 2 6 4    + 3 8 6    + 3 4 2    + 3 5 7
  4 2 3      5 6 1      5 3 5      5 3 0
```

```
  4 0 0      4 0 0      4 0 0      4 0 0
- 1 7 1    - 2 4 8    - 1 3 5    - 2 6 9
  2 2 9      1 5 2      2 6 5      1 3 1
```

```
  2 4 6      2 7 9      2 5 8      2 3 5
+ 2 8 6    + 2 5 2    + 4 7 5    + 2 7 8
  5 3 2      5 3 1      7 3 3      5 1 3
```

```
  5 0 0      5 0 0      7 0 0      7 0 0
- 1 4 8    - 2 3 9    - 1 5 7    - 2 6 3
  3 5 2      2 6 1      5 4 3      4 3 7
```

```
  3 6 4      3 7 7      3 1 5      3 8 6
+ 3 4 8    + 2 9 4    + 3 9 9    + 3 5 7
  7 1 2      6 7 1      7 1 4      7 4 3
```

Page 74

1. Add or subtract. Score ___/20   Time __:__

```
  4 1 3      5 2 7      3 2 8      3 0 4
+ 1 6 8    + 3 7 9    + 1 0 9    + 1 4 8
  5 8 1      9 0 6      4 3 7      4 5 2
```

```
  6 0 0      6 0 0      6 0 0      6 0 0
- 3 4 1    - 1 9 8    - 4 2 5    - 3 5 9
  2 5 9      4 0 2      1 7 5      2 4 1
```

```
  4 7 1      5 2 6      4 7 1      3 8 4
+ 3 9 9    + 1 8 5    + 2 4 9    + 3 3 7
  8 7 0      7 1 1      7 2 0      7 2 1
```

```
  7 0 0      7 0 0      7 0 0      7 0 0
- 3 6 9    - 3 9 4    - 6 1 5    - 4 9 6
  3 3 1      3 0 6        8 5      2 0 4
```

```
  5 1 6      6 3 1      5 4 8      6 8 3
+ 1 9 4    + 3 8 9    + 2 7 3    + 2 4 7
  7 1 0     1 0 2 0      8 2 1      9 3 0
```

Page 75

1. Add or subtract. Score ___/20   Time __:__

```
  6 4 1      5 9 7      4 7 9      6 3 6
+ 3 6 9    + 2 4 8    + 4 6 7    + 4 7 4
 1 0 1 0      8 4 5      9 4 6     1 1 1 0
```

```
  8 0 0      8 0 0      8 0 0      8 0 0
- 4 7 5    - 7 4 2    - 5 8 5    - 5 1 2
  3 2 5        5 8      2 1 5      2 8 8
```

```
  4 1 7      8 3 5      2 6 4      9 4 6
+ 4 8 7    + 1 7 8    + 4 9 9    + 1 3 7
  9 0 4     1 0 1 3      7 6 3     1 0 8 3
```

```
  9 0 0      9 0 0      9 0 0      9 0 0
- 3 8 7    - 5 1 3    - 6 4 5    - 7 2 6
  5 1 3      3 8 7      2 5 5      1 7 4
```

```
  2 7 4      1 0 7      4 8 2      9 0 4
+ 4 8 9    + 7 9 5    + 2 7 8    + 1 9 2
  7 6 3      9 0 2      7 6 0     1 0 9 6
```

Page 76

1. Add or subtract. Score ___/20   Time __:__

```
  7 5 8      6 7 8      8 9 9      4 7 5
+ 2 4 4    + 3 2 6    + 3 5 2    + 3 9 7
 1 0 0 2     1 0 0 4     1 2 5 1      8 7 2
```

```
  8 0 0      4 0 0      9 0 0      6 0 0
- 4 9 1    - 1 3 8    - 7 7 5    - 3 7 9
  3 0 9      2 6 2      1 2 5      2 2 1
```

```
  2 6 4      4 7 7      3 8 7      1 7 6
+ 8 6 9    + 5 3 5    + 7 6 9    + 8 3 8
 1 1 3 3     1 0 1 2     1 1 5 6     1 0 1 4
```

```
  5 0 0      7 0 0      9 0 0      3 0 0
- 4 1 6    - 3 6 8    - 5 2 3    - 1 8 7
    8 4      3 3 2      3 7 7      1 1 3
```

```
  5 3 4      4 9 7      3 6 8      3 4 4
+ 3 9 6    + 4 3 5    + 8 6 9    + 4 7 9
  9 3 0      9 3 2     1 2 3 7      8 2 3
```

Page 77

1. Add or subtract. Score ___/20   Time __:__

```
  7 5 4      6 7 5      8 7 9      4 5 5
+ 5 9 4    + 5 6 6    + 1 5 6    + 7 9 6
 1 3 4 8     1 2 4 1     1 0 3 5     1 2 5 1
```

```
  9 0 0      5 0 0      9 0 0      7 0 0
- 5 9 2    - 3 3 7    - 4 8 5    - 2 6 3
  3 0 8      1 6 3      4 1 5      4 3 7
```

```
  2 9 4      7 7 9      2 8 5      1 8 6
+ 5 6 7    + 5 4 5    + 7 7 9    + 4 3 4
  8 6 1     1 3 2 4     1 0 6 4      6 2 0
```

```
  6 0 0      8 0 0      6 0 0      8 0 0
- 3 9 5    - 2 8 8    - 4 8 3    - 5 8 5
  2 0 5      5 1 2      1 1 7      2 1 5
```

```
  5 6 4      8 9 6      2 6 5      3 5 4
+ 4 9 7    + 4 5 5    + 8 8 9    + 7 7 2
 1 0 6 1     1 3 5 1     1 1 5 4     1 1 2 6
```

Page 78

1. Add or subtract. Score ___/20   Time __:__

```
  3 1 5      9 8 7      6 9 8      3 0 2
+ 6 4 9    + 3 1 4    + 5 3 8    + 9 7 7
  9 6 4     1 3 0 1     1 2 3 6     1 2 7 9
```

```
  7 9 6      5 7 3      7 2 0      3 0 4
- 2 7 4    - 2 9 5    - 4 9 3    - 1 5 6
  5 2 2      2 7 8      2 2 7      1 4 8
```

```
  6 2 3      1 7 2      4 1 6      3 8 1
+ 2 8 7    + 8 9 8    + 8 0 4    + 1 4 9
  9 1 0     1 0 7 0     1 2 2 0      5 3 0
```

```
  8 0 3      7 0 6      5 0 7      7 0 9
- 1 8 7    - 2 9 7    - 2 7 6    - 4 3 9
  6 1 6      4 0 9      2 3 1      2 7 0
```

```
  5 8 9      3 4 6      5 1 2      6 7 2
+ 9 7 6    + 8 7 3    + 9 7 9    + 2 4 7
 1 5 6 5     1 2 1 9     1 4 9 1     1 4 6 9
```

Page 79

1. Add or subtract. Score ___/20 Time __:__

614 + 689 = 1303	997 + 215 = 1212	678 + 746 = 1424	382 + 258 = 640
892 − 234 = 658	812 − 295 = 517	621 − 433 = 188	801 − 146 = 655
573 + 168 = 741	723 + 195 = 918	315 + 485 = 800	549 + 938 = 1487
903 − 385 = 518	716 − 498 = 218	802 − 246 = 556	704 − 379 = 325
476 + 278 = 754	398 + 695 = 1093	497 + 524 = 1021	483 + 609 = 1092

Page 80

1. Add or subtract. Score ___/20 Time __:__

368 + 145 = 513	359 + 193 = 552	882 + 874 = 1756	768 + 345 = 1113
725 − 487 = 238	308 − 189 = 119	783 − 479 = 304	976 − 588 = 388
277 + 718 = 995	879 + 144 = 1023	163 + 368 = 531	992 + 754 = 1746
507 − 175 = 332	901 − 235 = 666	603 − 154 = 449	805 − 358 = 447
535 + 269 = 804	587 + 336 = 923	256 + 467 = 723	645 + 335 = 980

Page 81

1. Add or subtract. Score ___/20 Time __:__

378 + 567 = 945	893 + 673 = 1566	842 + 902 = 1744	467 + 568 = 1035
936 − 589 = 347	535 − 167 = 368	846 − 357 = 489	987 − 498 = 489
685 + 395 = 1080	967 + 784 = 1751	483 + 589 = 1072	696 + 264 = 960
831 − 393 = 438	905 − 485 = 420	785 − 299 = 486	791 − 487 = 304
314 + 589 = 903	625 + 678 = 1303	483 + 869 = 1352	689 + 946 = 1635

Page 82

1. Subtract. Score ___/20 Time __:__

1000 − 225 = 775	1000 − 156 = 844	1000 − 734 = 266	1000 − 519 = 481
1000 − 172 = 828	1000 − 693 = 307	1000 − 758 = 242	1000 − 472 = 528
1000 − 585 = 415	1000 − 459 = 541	1000 − 531 = 469	1000 − 716 = 284
1000 − 665 = 335	1000 − 486 = 514	1000 − 944 = 56	1000 − 379 = 621
1000 − 674 = 326	1000 − 431 = 569	1000 − 289 = 711	1000 − 745 = 255

Made in the USA
Monee, IL
25 August 2020